Math in Focus®

Singapore Math®
by Marshall Cavendish

Student Edition

Program Consultant and Author
Dr. Fong Ho Kheong

Authors
Gan Kee Soon
Chelvi Ramakrishnan

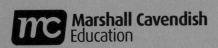

Marshall Cavendish
Education

U.S. Distributor

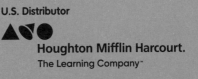

Houghton Mifflin Harcourt.
The Learning Company™

Grade
5B

Contents

Chapter

 Volume

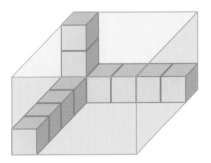

Line Plots and the Coordinate Plane

Polygons

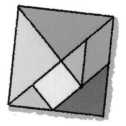

 Ratio

Chapter Opener **147**

▶ Hands-on Activity

Chapter

10 Percent

Chapter Opener

What does percent mean? How can you represent a percent in different ways? How can percents be used in real world situations?

RECALL PRIOR KNOWLEDGE

Writing fractions with a denominator of 100 as a decimal • Finding equivalent fractions using multiplication • Simplifying fractions using division • Finding equivalent fractions and decimals

▶ Hands-on Activity

Manipulative List

Connecting cubes   Transparent counters

Preface

Welcome!

Math in Focus® is a program that puts **you** at the center of an exciting learning experience! This experience is all about helping you to build skills and math ideas that make sense, sharing your thinking to deepen your understanding, and learning to become a strong and confident problem solver!

What's in your book?

Each chapter in this book begins with a real-world example of the math topic you are about to learn.

In each chapter, you will see the following features:

THINK introduces a problem for the whole section, to get you thinking creatively and critically. You may not be able to answer the problem right away but you can come back to it a few times as you work through the section.

ENGAGE introduces tasks that link what you already know with what you will be learning next. The tasks will have you exploring and discussing math concepts with your classmates.

LEARN introduces you to new math concepts through a Concrete-Pictorial-Abstract (C-P-A) approach, using examples and activities.

Hands-on Activity provides you with the experience of working very closely with your classmates. These Hands-On Activities allow you to become more confident in what you have learned and help you to uncover new concepts.

TRY provides you with the opportunity to practice what you are learning, with support and guidance.

INDEPENDENT PRACTICE allows you to work on different kinds of problems and apply the concepts and skills you have learned to solve these problems on your own.

Additional features include:

RECALL PRIOR KNOWLEDGE	Math Talk	MATH SHARING	GAME
Helps you recall related concepts you learned before, accompanied by practice questions	Invites you to explain your reasoning and communicate your ideas to your classmates and teachers	Encourages you to create strategies, discover methods, and share them with your classmates and teachers using mathematical language	Helps you to really master the concepts you learned, through fun partner games
LET'S EXPLORE	**MATH JOURNAL**	**PUT ON YOUR THINKING CAP!**	**CHAPTER WRAP-UP**
Extends your learning through investigation	Allows you to reflect on your learning when you write down your thoughts about the concepts learned	Challenges you to apply the concepts to solve problems in different ways	Summarizes your learning in a flow chart and helps you to make connections within the chapter
CHAPTER REVIEW	**Assessment Prep**	**PERFORMANCE TASK**	**STEAM**
Provides you with a lot of practice in the concepts learned	Prepares you for state tests with assessment-type problems	Assesses your learning through problems that allow you to demonstrate your understanding and knowledge	Promotes collaboration with your classmates through interesting projects that allow you to use math in creative ways

Let's begin your exciting learning journey with us! Are you ready?

Volume

How can I find the volume of water this glass box can hold?

How can you measure the amount of space in a box or container? What units can we use?

Name: _____ Date: _____

Understanding three-dimensional figures

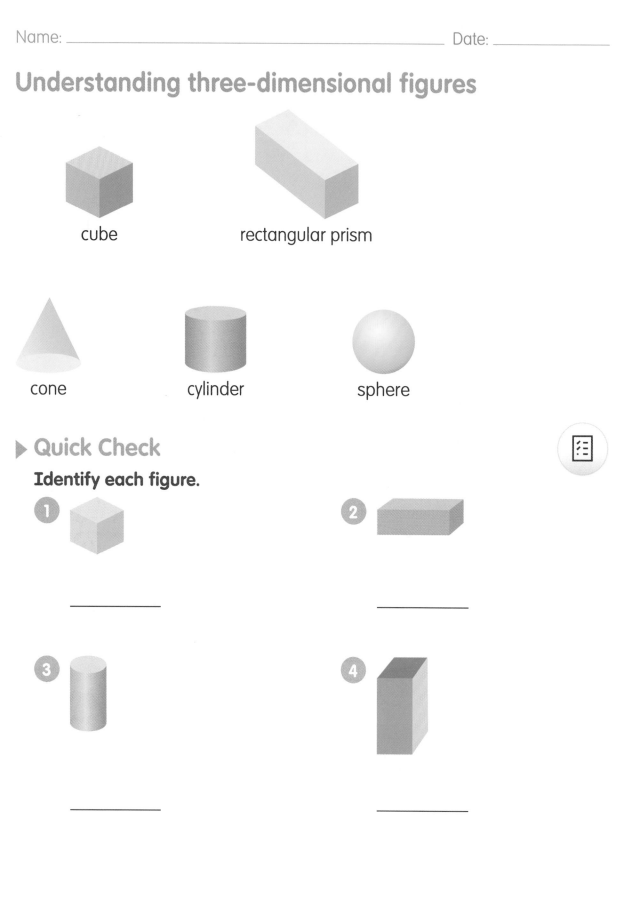

cube

rectangular prism

cone

cylinder

sphere

▶ **Quick Check**

Identify each figure.

1 _____

2 _____

3 _____

4 _____

Measuring volume and capacity

Add more chocolate milk.

Pour all the chocolate milk into a measuring cup.

The container is partly filled with chocolate milk. The volume of chocolate milk in the container is 400 milliliters.

The container is completely filled with chocolate milk.

The capacity of the container is 900 milliliters.

Liters and milliliters are units of volume.
1 L = 1,000 mL

Volume is the amount of liquid in a container. Capacity is the amount of liquid a container can hold.

▶ **Quick Check**

Fill in each blank.

⑤ 6 L = _____ mL

⑥ 5,000 mL = _____ L

⑦ 2,019 mL = _____ L _____ mL

⑧ 1 L 268 mL = _____ mL

9. The capacity of a pitcher is 8 liters. The pitcher is filled to the brim with water. Find the volume of water in the pitcher in milliliters.

10. The fuel tank of a car is half full. The volume of fuel in the tank is 25 liters. Find the capacity of the tank.

Name: _____ Date: _____

1 Building Solids Using Unit Cubes

Learning Objectives:
- Use unit cubes to build solids.
- Determine the number of unit cubes in an irregular solid.
- Recognize that the volume of a solid is the amount of space it occupies.

New Vocabulary
unit cube
congruent
edge

THINK

The solid is made up of identical cubes.

How many cubes make up each solid?
Dismantle the solid and build four other different solids.

ENGAGE

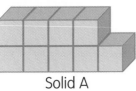

Solid A

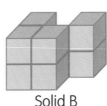

Solid B

Solid A and Solid B are made up of unit cubes.
How many unit cubes are there in each solid?
Explain how you get the answers in two different ways.

LEARN Build solids using unit cubes

1. The solid shown is a unit cube.
   It is a cube in which all the edges are 1 unit long.

   A cube has 6 square faces.
   All its faces are congruent.
   All congruent faces have the same shape and size.
   It has 12 edges.
   The lengths of all its edges are equal.

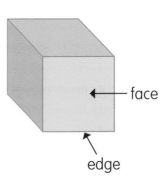

← face

edge

2 This is another unit cube.

You can build solids using unit cubes.
This solid is made up of 2 unit cubes.

Hands-on Activity Using unit cubes to build different solids

Work in pairs.

1 Use unit cubes to build each solid.

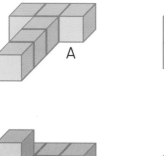
A

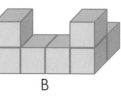
B

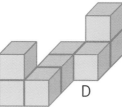
C

D

2 Count the number of cubes used to build each solid.

a   Solid A is made up of _____ unit cubes.

b   Solid B is made up of _____ unit cubes.

c   Solid C is made up of _____ unit cubes.

d   Solid D is made up of _____ unit cubes.

TRY Practice building solids using unit cubes

Fill in each blank.

1 Each of these solids is made up of _____ unit cubes.

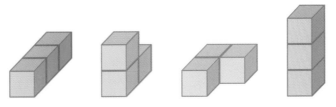

2 This solid is made up of _____ unit cubes.

ENGAGE

Look at the following pairs of objects in your classroom.
a   a chair and a desk
b   a book and a pencil
c   a glue stick and a water bottle
Which object takes up more space? How do you know? Explain to your partner.

LEARN Compare solids

1

The watermelon takes up more space than the orange in the refrigerator.

This is because the watermelon has a greater volume than the orange.

> The **volume** of a solid is the amount of space it occupies.

 You can compare objects to find which occupies more space.

tennis ball

balloon

The balloon has a greater volume than the tennis ball.
The tennis ball has less volume than the balloon.

TRY Practice comparing solids

Circle the object with the greater volume.

jar of jam

shoe box

Circle the object with less volume.

can of apple juice

soccer ball

INDEPENDENT PRACTICE

Find the number of cubes used to build each solid.

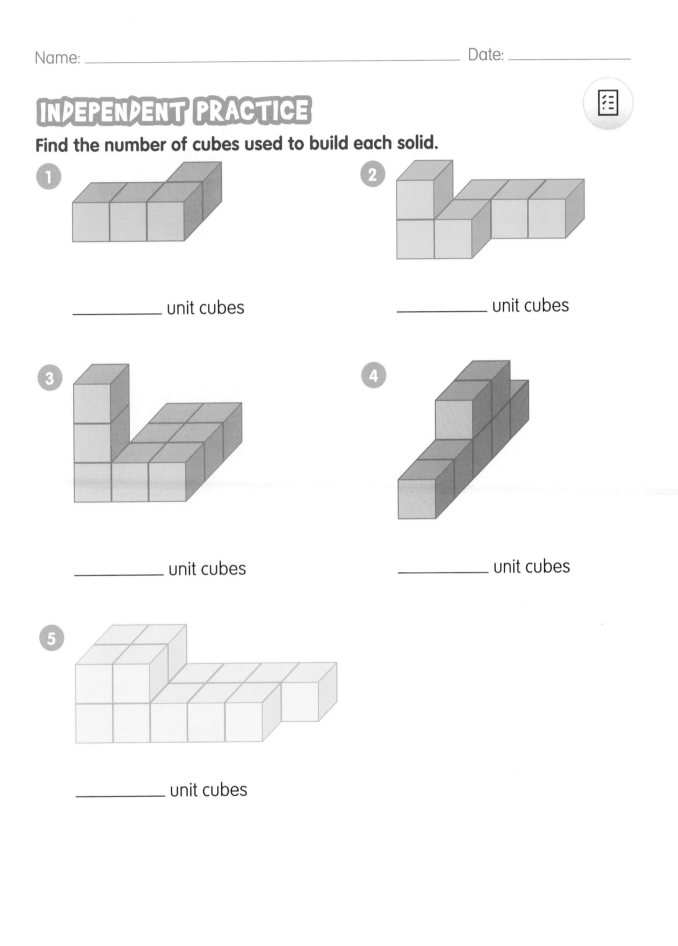

1

_____ unit cubes

2

_____ unit cubes

3

_____ unit cubes

4

_____ unit cubes

5

_____ unit cubes

Circle the object with the greater volume.

6

softball

football

7

gift box

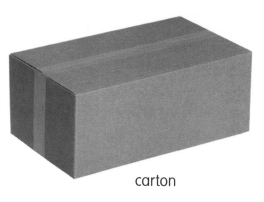

carton

Circle the object with the smaller volume.

8

basketball

can

Understanding and Measuring Volume

Learning Objectives:
- Find the volume of a solid made up of unit cubes.
- Find the volumes of cubes and rectangular prisms.

THINK

The figure is made up of two rectangular prisms.
Explain how you would find the volume of the figure.

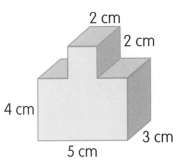

2 cm
2 cm
4 cm
5 cm
3 cm

ENGAGE

Use 20 to form a solid with more than two layers. Sketch your solid. How could you find the volume of your solid without counting each cube individually? Explain your thinking.

LEARN Find and compare the volume of solids in cubic units

1. The volume of a cube or rectangular prism is the number of cubic units needed to make it.

   This is a unit cube. It has a volume of 1 cubic unit.

   Count the number of unit cubes used to make the cube.

    top layer
   bottom layer
   →

   cube

   This cube is made up of 8 unit cubes.
   Its volume is 8 cubic units.

2

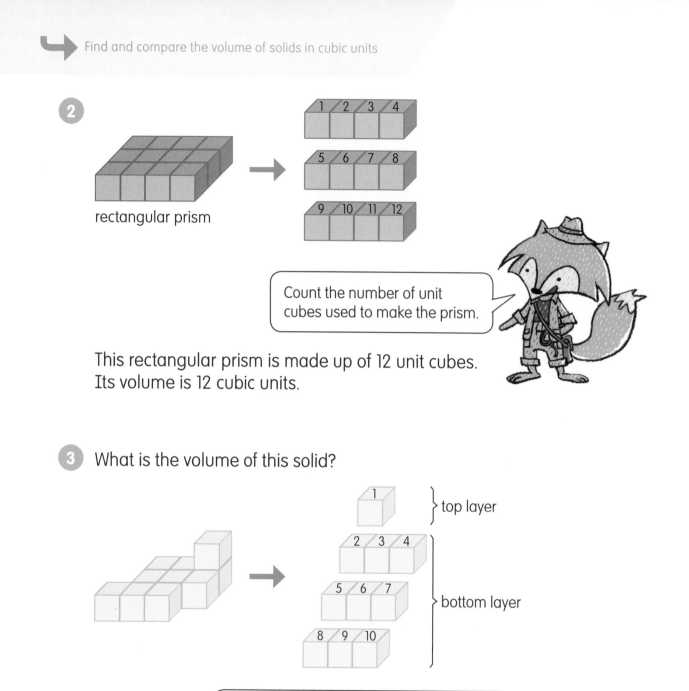

rectangular prism

Count the number of unit cubes used to make the prism.

This rectangular prism is made up of 12 unit cubes.
Its volume is 12 cubic units.

3 What is the volume of this solid?

top layer

bottom layer

Count the number of unit cubes in the solid to find out its volume.

This solid is made up of 10 unit cubes.
Its volume is 10 cubic units.

Hands-on Activity Discovering that different solids can have the same volume

Work in pairs.

(1) Build the rectangular prism using 12 unit cubes.

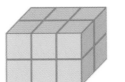

The volume of the rectangular prism is _____ cubic units.

(2) Rearrange the cubes to build solid A.

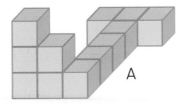

A

The volume of solid A is _____ cubic units.

(3) Rearrange the cubes to build solid B.

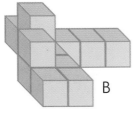

B

The volume of solid B is _____ cubic units.

(4) Build two other solids using 12 unit cubes.
What is the volume of each solid? What do you notice about the volume of these different solids?

TRY Practice finding and comparing the volume of solids in cubic units

Each prism is made up of unit cubes. Find the volume of each prism.

1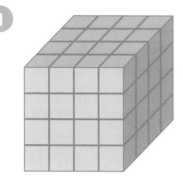

1 layer has _____ unit cubes.

4 layers have _____ unit cubes.

Volume of the prism

= _____ cubic units

2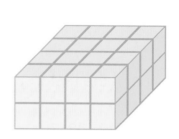

1 layer has _____ unit cubes.

2 layers have _____ unit cubes.

Volume of the prism

= _____ cubic units

Each solid is made up of unit cubes. Find the volume of each solid.

3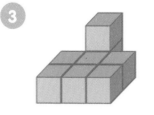

Volume of solid

= _____ cubic units

4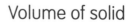

Volume of solid

= _____ cubic units

ENGAGE

The area of the base of a rectangular prism is found by multiplying its length by its width. It is measured in square units.

Use 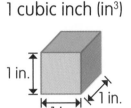 to make four different rectangular prisms, each with a base area of 12 square units. Use them to build rectangular prisms with more cubes. What are the possible numbers of cubes in your rectangular prisms?

LEARN Find the volume of a solid in cubic units

1. These are some units of measurements for volume.

1 cubic centimeter (cm³)

The length of each edge of the cube is 1 centimeter.
Volume of the cube = 1 cm³

1 cubic inch (in³)

The length of each edge of the cube is 1 inch.
Volume of the cube = 1 in³

1 cubic foot (ft³)

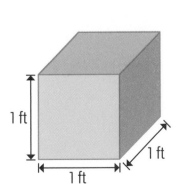

The length of each edge of the cube is 1 foot.
Volume of the cube = 1 ft³

1 cubic meter (m³)

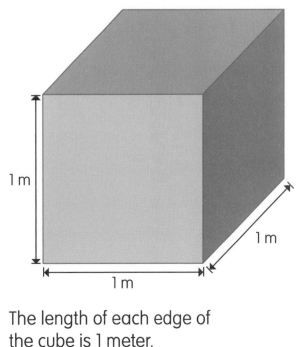

The length of each edge of the cube is 1 meter.
Volume of the cube = 1 m³

2 The rectangular prism is made up of sixteen 1-inch cubes.

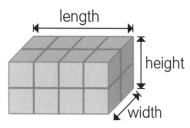

Length = 4 in.
Width = 2 in.
Height = 2 in.
Volume of the rectangular prism = 16 in³

TRY Practice finding the volume of a solid in cubic units

Fill in each blank.

1 The rectangular prism is made up of 1-foot cubes.

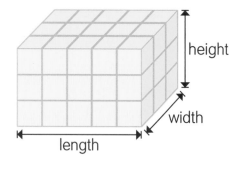

Length = _____ ft

Width = _____ ft

Height = _____ ft

Volume = _____ ft³

2 The rectangular prism is made up of 1-meter cubes.

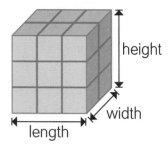

Length = _____ m

Width = _____ m

Height = _____ m

Volume = _____ m³

3 **Find the volume of each solid, then compare their volumes.**

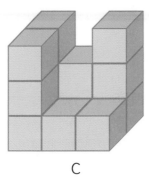

A

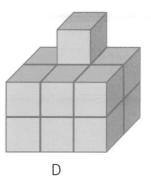

B

Volume of A = _____ in³   Volume of B = _____ in³

_____ has a greater volume than _____.

4 **Find the volume of each solid, then compare their volumes.**

C

D

Volume of C = _____ in³   Volume of D = _____ in³

What do you observe about the volumes of solids C and D?

_____

© 2020 Marshall Cavendish Education Pte Ltd

ENGAGE

With a partner, find and sketch three different examples of rectangular prisms found in your classroom. Use two different methods to find the volume of each prism that you sketched.

LEARN Find the volume of a rectangular prism

1 This is a rectangular prism. All the faces of a rectangular prism are rectangles.

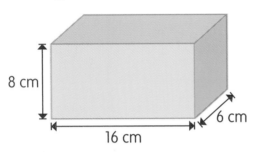

Math Talk
Explain if two opposite faces of a rectangular prism can be squares.

The length of the rectangular prism is 16 centimeters.
Its width is 6 centimeters.
Its height is 8 centimeters.

2 This rectangular prism is made up of 1-centimeter cubes.

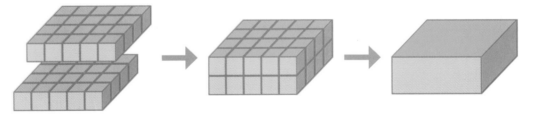

The length of the prism is 5 centimeters.
The width of the prism is 4 centimeters.
The height of the prism is 2 centimeters.

In the bottom layer, there are 5 × 4 = 20 1-centimeter cubes.
In two layers, there are 20 × 2 = 5 × 4 × 2 = 40 1-centimeter cubes.

Volume of the rectangular prism = 5 × 4 × 2
    = 40 cm³

Volume of a rectangular prism = length × width × height

3 A rectangular prism measures 15 inches long, 8 inches wide, and 6 inches high. Find its volume.

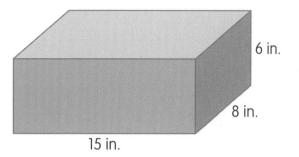

6 in.

8 in.

15 in.

Volume of the rectangular prism = length × width × height
= 15 × 8 × 6
= 720 in.^{3}

4 A cube has edges 6 centimeters long. Find its volume.

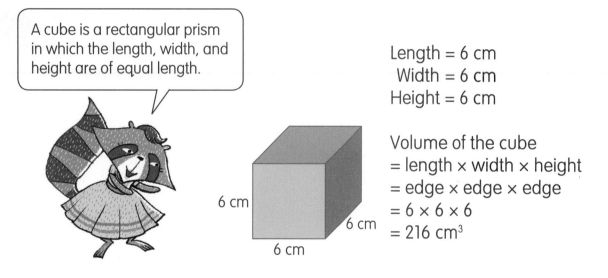

A cube is a rectangular prism in which the length, width, and height are of equal length.

6 cm

6 cm

6 cm

Length = 6 cm
Width = 6 cm
Height = 6 cm

Volume of the cube
= length × width × height
= edge × edge × edge
= 6 × 6 × 6
= 216 cm^3

Hands-on Activity Building prisms layer by layer to establish the formula for volume of a rectangular prism

Work in pairs.

1 Using 1-centimeter cubes, build rectangular prism A as shown.

Rectangular prism A

Volume of rectangular prism A = _____ cm^3

(2) Ask your partner to add another layer to build rectangular prism B.

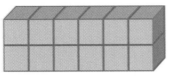

Rectangular prism B

Volume of rectangular prism B = _____ cm³

(3) Build rectangular prism C.

Rectangular prism C

Volume of rectangular prism C = _____ cm³

What is the length, width, and height of rectangular prism C?

(4) **Mathematical Habit 7** **Make use of structure**
What do you notice about the number of layers and the height of the rectangular prism? What is the relationship between the volume of the rectangular prism and its length, width, and height?

TRY Practice finding volume of a rectangular prism

Fill in each blank.

1 The rectangular prism is made up of 1-inch cubes.

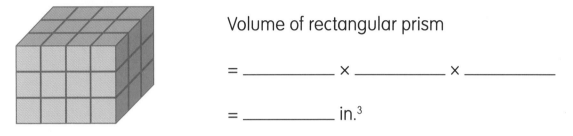

Volume of rectangular prism

= _____ × _____ × _____

= _____ in.³

Find the volume of each solid figure.

2

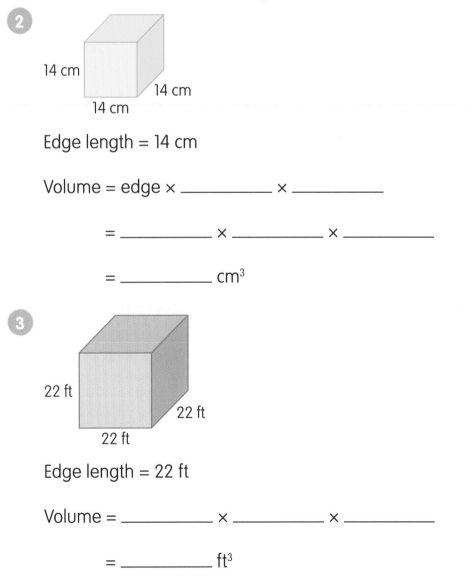

14 cm

14 cm

14 cm

Edge length = 14 cm

Volume = edge × _____ × _____

= _____ × _____ × _____

= _____ cm³

3

22 ft

22 ft

22 ft

Edge length = 22 ft

Volume = _____ × _____ × _____

= _____ ft³

4

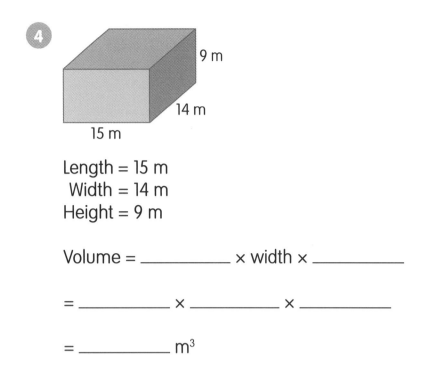

9 m

14 m

15 m

Length = 15 m

Width = 14 m

Height = 9 m

Volume = _____ × width × _____

= _____ × _____ × _____

= _____ m³

© 2020 Marshall Cavendish Education Pte Ltd

MATH SHARING

Mathematical Habit 8 Look for patterns

A rectangular prism has its length, width, and height in whole centimeters. The volume of the rectangular prism is 120 cubic centimeters and its length is 5 centimeters.

What are the possible values of the width and height of the rectangular prism? Fill in the table.

Length (cm)	Width (cm)	Height (cm)	Volume (cm³)
5			
5			
5			
5			

Discuss with your partner what you noticed about rectangular prisms with equal volumes.

INDEPENDENT PRACTICE

Each solid is made up of unit cubes. Find the volume of each solid.

1

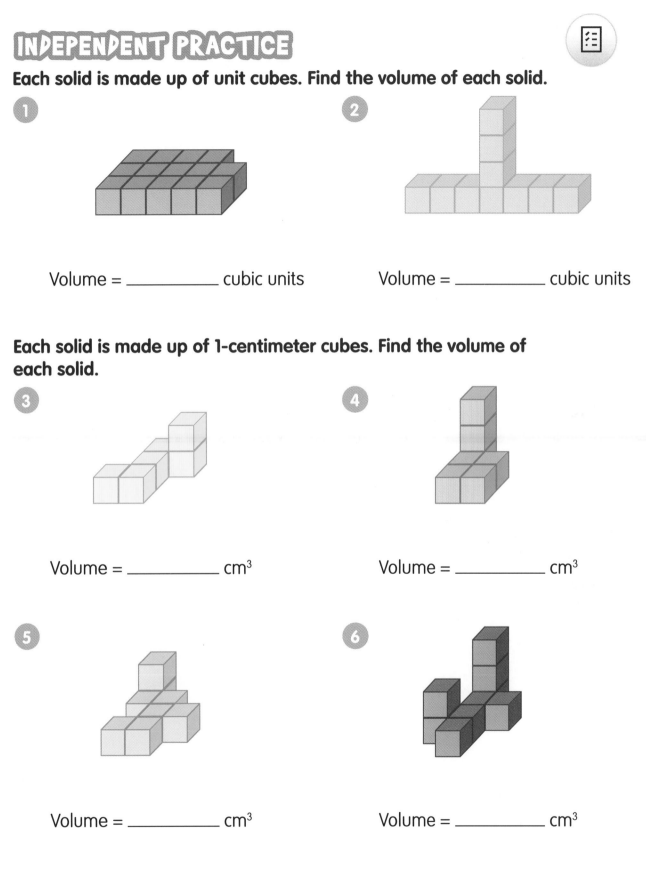

Volume = _____ cubic units

2

Volume = _____ cubic units

Each solid is made up of 1-centimeter cubes. Find the volume of each solid.

3

Volume = _____ cm³

4

Volume = _____ cm³

5

Volume = _____ cm³

6

Volume = _____ cm³

Find the volume of each solid. Then compare their volumes.

7 Each rectangular prism is built using 1-inch cubes.

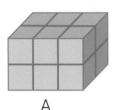

A

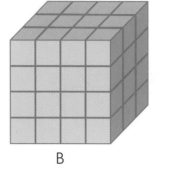

B

Length = _____ in.

Width = _____ in.

Height = _____ in.

Volume = _____ in.^{3}

Length = _____ in.

Width = _____ in.

Height = _____ in.

Volume = _____ in.^{3}

A has _____ (a greater / less) volume than B.

8 Each solid is built using 1-foot cubes.

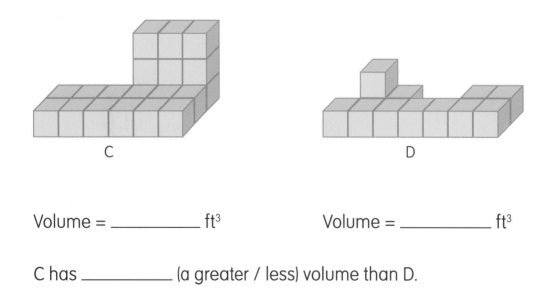

C

D

Volume = _____ ft^3

Volume = _____ ft^3

C has _____ (a greater / less) volume than D.

Each solid is made up of 1-centimeter cubes. Find the volume of each solid.

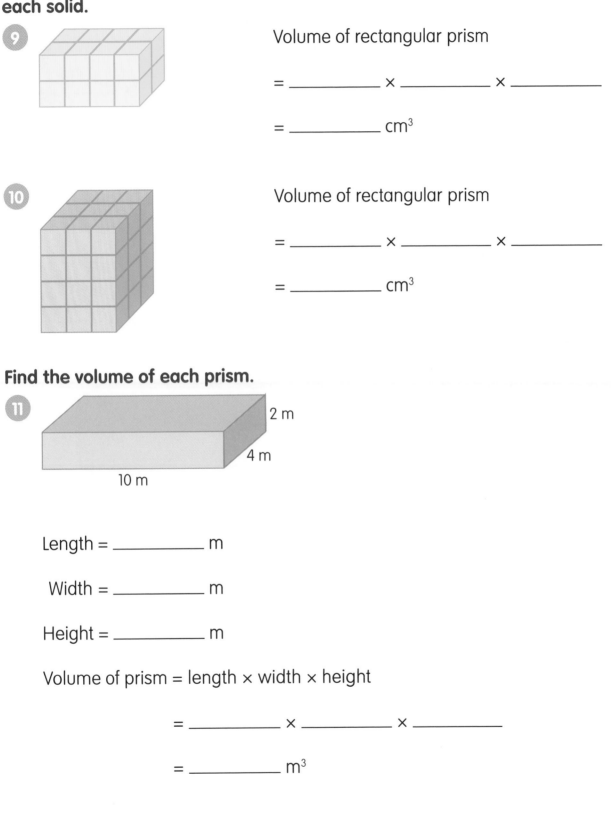

9

Volume of rectangular prism

= _____ × _____ × _____

= _____ cm³

10

Volume of rectangular prism

= _____ × _____ × _____

= _____ cm³

Find the volume of each prism.

11

2 m

4 m

10 m

Length = _____ m

Width = _____ m

Height = _____ m

Volume of prism = length × width × height

= _____ × _____ × _____

= _____ m³

12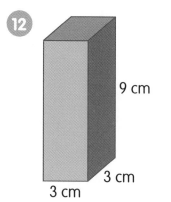

9 cm

3 cm

3 cm

Volume of prism
= length × width × height

= _____ × _____ × _____

= _____ m³

13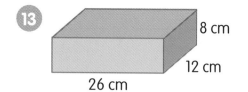

8 cm

12 cm

26 cm

14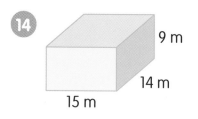

9 m

14 m

15 m

15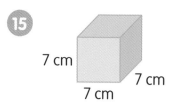

7 cm

7 cm

7 cm

Name: _____   Date: _____

3 Real-World Problems: Volume of Rectangular Prisms

Learning Objectives:
- Use a formula to find the volume of a rectangular prism.
- Find the capacity of a rectangular container.
- Solve word problems on volume of rectangular prisms and liquids.

THINK

A rectangular container measuring 12 centimeters by 15 centimeters by 18 centimeters is $\frac{2}{3}$ filled with water. All the water is then poured into another rectangular container until it is $\frac{2}{5}$ full. Find two possible dimensions of the second container.

ENGAGE

1. A rectangular container measures 20 cm by 10 cm by 15 cm. The container is completely filled with water. What is the volume of the water in the container?

2. A rectangular glass box is completely filled with water. The volume of the water is 1,800 cubic centimeters. Find two possible dimensions of the box.

LEARN Convert volumes of liquid

1. A glass tank measuring 10 centimeters by 10 centimeters by 10 centimeters is completely filled with water.

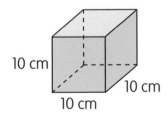

10 cm
10 cm
10 cm

Volume of water in the glass tank
= 10 × 10 × 10
= 1,000 cm^3

All the water in the glass tank is then poured into a 1-liter beaker.

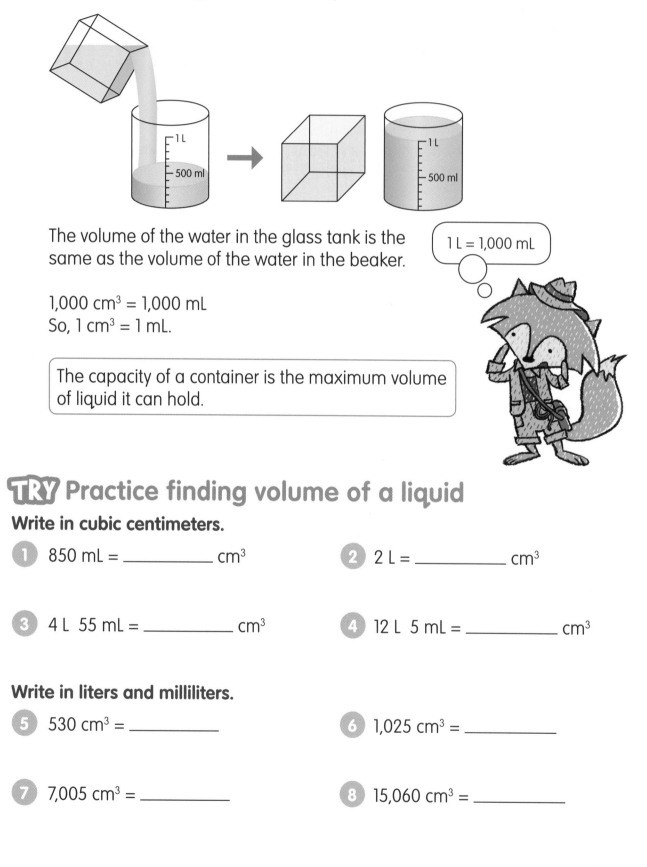

The volume of the water in the glass tank is the same as the volume of the water in the beaker.

1 L = 1,000 mL

1,000 cm³ = 1,000 mL
So, 1 cm³ = 1 mL.

The capacity of a container is the maximum volume of liquid it can hold.

TRY Practice finding volume of a liquid

Write in cubic centimeters.

1 850 mL = _____ cm³

2 2 L = _____ cm³

3 4 L 55 mL = _____ cm³

4 12 L 5 mL = _____ cm³

Write in liters and milliliters.

5 530 cm³ = _____

6 1,025 cm³ = _____

7 7,005 cm³ = _____

8 15,060 cm³ = _____

ENGAGE

a Use 12 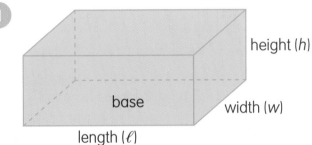 to make a rectangular prism. Find the length, width, and height of the rectangular prism. How are the three measurements and the volume related?

b Repeat **a** with 18, 24, and 36 ▪. Do you see a pattern? Explain to your partner.

LEARN Use a formula to find the volume of a rectangular prism

1

height (*h*)

base

width (*w*)

length (*ℓ*)

This is a rectangular prism of length *ℓ*, width *w*, and height *h*.

Volume of a rectangular prism = length × width × height

If *V* is the volume, then

$$V = ℓ \times w \times h$$

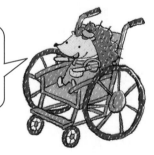

V = *ℓ* × *w* × *h* is a formula for the volume of a rectangular prism.

Since *ℓ* × *w* is the area of the base, the volume of a rectangular prism is the area of base × *h*.

If *B* is the area of the base, then

$$V = B \times h$$

V = *B* × *h* is another formula for the volume of a rectangular prism.

Find the volume of the rectangular prism.

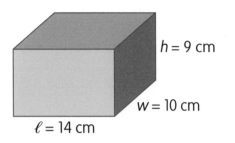

$h = 9$ cm

$w = 10$ cm

$\ell = 14$ cm

Length = 14 cm
Width = 10 cm
Height = 9 cm

$V = \ell \times w \times h$
$= 14 \times 10 \times 9$
$= 1{,}260$

The volume of the prism is 1,260 cubic centimeters.

2 Find the volume of the rectangular prism.

$h = 3$ cm

$B = 98$ cm^2

Area of base = 98 cm^2
Height = 3 cm

$V = B \times h$
$= 98 \times 3$
$= 294$

The volume of the prism is 294 cubic centimeters.

TRY Practice using a formula to find the volume of a rectangular prism

Find the volume of each rectangular prism.

①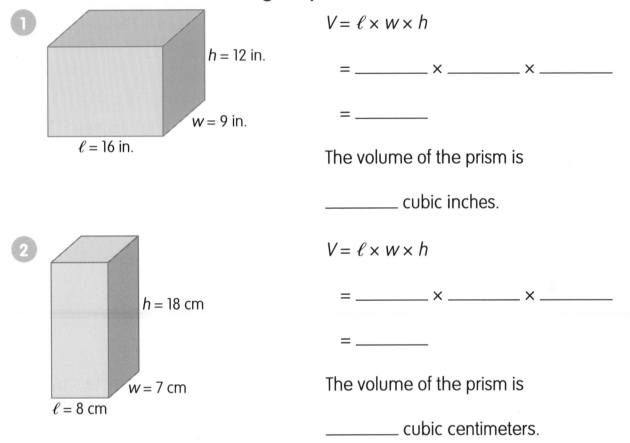

$V = \ell \times w \times h$

= _____ × _____ × _____

= _____

The volume of the prism is

_____ cubic inches.

②

$V = \ell \times w \times h$

= _____ × _____ × _____

= _____

The volume of the prism is

_____ cubic centimeters.

Find the volume of each rectangular prism.

③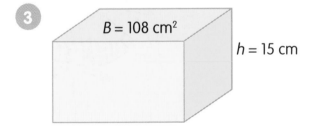

Area of base = 108 cm²
Height = 15 cm

$V = B \times h$

= _____ × _____

= _____

The volume of the prism is

_____ cubic centimeters.

4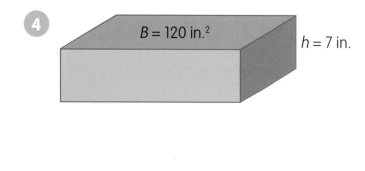

Area of base = 120 in²
Height = 7 in.

$V = B \times h$

= _____ × _____

= _____

The volume of the prism is

_____ cubic inches.

ENGAGE

a A cube-shaped fish tank has a capacity of 512,000 cubic centimeters. What are the dimensions of the tank?

b A pail has a capacity of 20 liters. How many pails can be used to fill the fish tank completely? Explain your thinking.

LEARN Solve one-step word problems

1 A rectangular container measures 15 centimeters by 10 centimeters by 8 centimeters. It is completely filled with water. How many liters and milliliters of water are in the container?

STEP **1** What is the length, width, and height of the container?
How much is the container filled?
What do I need to find?

STEP **2** Think of a plan.
I can use a formula.

STEP **3** Carry out the plan.

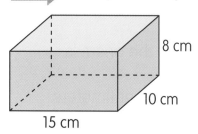

Volume of water in the container = 15 × 10 × 8
= 1,200 cm³
= 1,200 mL
= 1 L 200 mL

There are 1 liter 200 milliliters of water in the container.

© 2020 Marshall Cavendish Education Pte Ltd

Check the answer.

I can work backwards to check my answer.

> 1 L 200 mL = 1,200 mL
> 1,200 ÷ 10 = 120
> 120 ÷ 8 = 15
> The product of the length, width, and height
> is 1,200 cm³. So, my answer is correct.

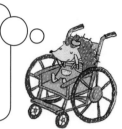

TRY Practice solving one-step word problems

Solve.

1. A box measures 26 centimeters by 15 centimeters by 12 centimeters. What is the capacity of the box? Give your answer in liters and milliliters.

   Capacity of the box = _____ × _____ × _____

   = _____ cm³

   = _____ mL

   = _____ L _____ mL

   The capacity of the box is _____ liters _____ milliliters.

2. The base area of a rectangular container is 12 square feet. The height of the container is 2 feet. What is the capacity of the container?

   Capacity of the container = _____ × _____

   = _____ ft³

   The capacity of the container is _____ cubic feet.

A rectangular container measuring 12 centimeters by 5 centimeters by 5 centimeters is $\frac{1}{2}$ filled with water. Water from a tap flows into the container at 50 milliliters per second. How long will it take to fill up the container?

Explain to your partner how you have found your answer.

LEARN Solve two-step word problems

1. Each edge of an aquarium is 15 centimeters long. It contains 1.25 liters of water. How much more water is needed to fill the aquarium completely? Give your answer in liters. (1 L = 1,000 cm³)

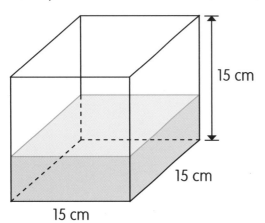

15 cm

15 cm

15 cm

Capacity of the aquarium = 15 × 15 × 15
$\qquad$ = 3,375 cm³
$\qquad$ = 3,375 mL
$\qquad$ = 3.375 L

Volume of water in the aquarium = 1.25 L

Volume of water needed to fill the aquarium completely
= 3.375 − 1.25
= 2.125 L

2.125 liters of water are needed to fill the aquarium completely.

TRY Practice solving two-step word problems

Solve.

1. There are 1.75 liters of water in the rectangular container shown. How much more water is needed to fill the container completely? Give your answer in liters. (1 L = 1,000 cm³)

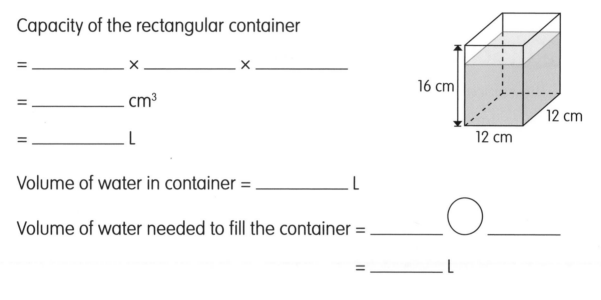

Capacity of the rectangular container

= _____ × _____ × _____

= _____ cm³

= _____ L

Volume of water in container = _____ L

Volume of water needed to fill the container = _____ ◯ _____

= _____ L

_____ liter of water is needed to fill the container completely.

2. A rectangular tank measuring 38 centimeters by 24 centimeters by 15 centimeters is filled with water up to $\frac{3}{5}$ of its height. Then, some water is poured out of the tank. The amount of water left is 4,560 cubic centimeters. How many milliliters of water are poured out of the tank?

Volume of water in tank

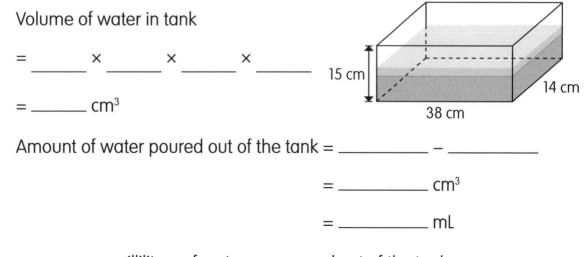

= _____ × _____ × _____ × _____

= _____ cm³

Amount of water poured out of the tank = _____ – _____

= _____ cm³

= _____ mL

_____ milliliters of water are poured out of the tank.

ENGAGE

Mateo was baking a cake. The recipe stated that the cake batter would completely fill a rectangular pan that measured 16 inches by 24 inches by 3 inches. He decided to use two smaller rectangular pans that each measured 8 inches by 12 inches by 3 inches instead. Would the cake batter fit into the two smaller pans? Justify your reasoning.

LEARN Solve three-step word problems

1 The cubical tank on the left is $\frac{2}{3}$ full. The water in it is then poured into the rectangular tank on the right until it is full. How much water is left in the cubical tank? Give your answer in milliliters. (1 cm³ = 1 mL)

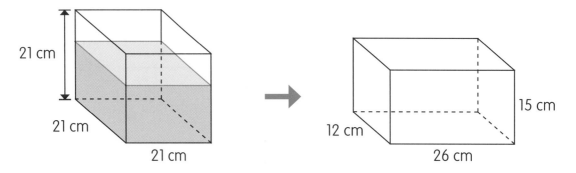

Volume of water in the cubical tank $= \frac{2}{3} \times 21 \times 21 \times 21$
$= 6,174 \text{ cm}^3$
$= 6,174 \text{ mL}$

Capacity of the rectangular tank $= 26 \times 12 \times 15$
$= 4,680 \text{ cm}^3$
$= 4,680 \text{ mL}$

Volume of water left in the cubical tank $= 6,174 - 4,680$
$= 1,494 \text{ mL}$

The cubical tank has 1,494 milliliters of water left.

TRY Practice solving three-step word problems

Solve.

1. A rectangular tank measuring 32 centimeters by 26 centimeters by 16 centimeters is $\frac{3}{4}$ filled with water. The water is then poured into a cubical tank of edge 19 centimeters until it is full. How many liters of water are left in the rectangular tank?

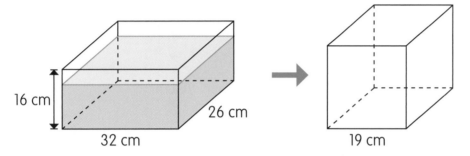

16 cm
32 cm
26 cm
19 cm

Capacity of water in the rectangular tank

= _____ × _____ × _____ × _____

= _____ cm³

Capacity of cubical tank

= _____ × _____ × _____

= _____ cm³

Amount of water left in the rectangular tank

= _____ − _____

= _____ cm³

= _____ mL

= _____ L

_____ liters of water are left in the rectangular tank.

2 A rectangular tank shown is filled with water to $\frac{1}{4}$ of its height. Water from a tap flows into the tank at 2.5 liters a minute. How much water is in the tank after 5 minutes? Give your answer in liters. (1 L = 1000 cm³)

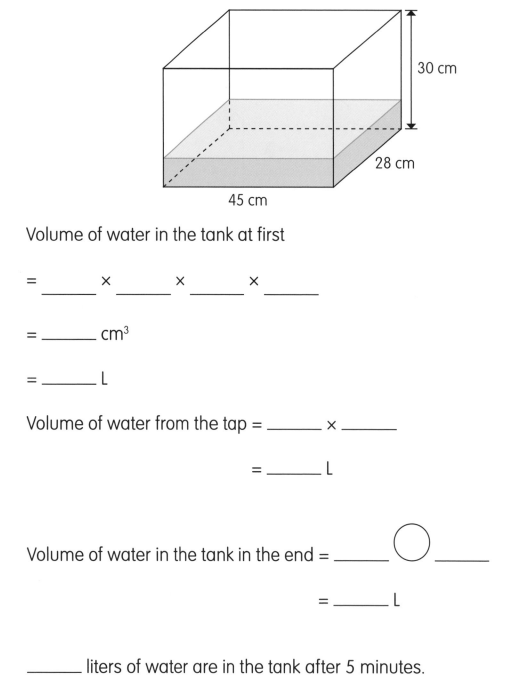

30 cm

28 cm

45 cm

Volume of water in the tank at first

= _____ × _____ × _____ × _____

= _____ cm³

= _____ L

Volume of water from the tap = _____ × _____

= _____ L

Volume of water in the tank in the end = _____ ◯ _____

= _____ L

_____ liters of water are in the tank after 5 minutes.

INDEPENDENT PRACTICE

Solve.

1 Find the volume of the rectangular solid prism.

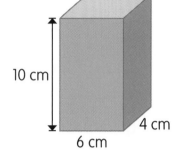

2 Find the volume of water in the rectangular tank in milliliters.

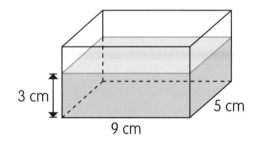

3 Find the volume of water in the rectangular tank in liters and milliliters.

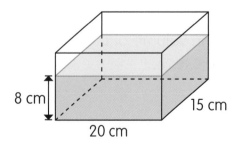

Solve.

4 A rectangular prism is 29 centimeters long, 15 centimeters wide, and 4 centimeters high. Find its volume.

5 A rectangular prism is 42 inches long, 32 inches wide, and 26 inches high. Find its volume.

6 A rectangular tub measures 15 meters by 11 meters by 5 meters. Find its capacity in cubic meters.

7 Find the volume of a cube with an edge length of 21 feet. Give your answer in cubic feet.

8 A rectangular tank, 28 centimeters by 18 centimeters by 12 centimeters, is filled with water completely. Then, 0.78 liter of water is drained from the tank. How much water is left in the tank? Give your answer in milliliters. (1 L = 1,000 cm³)

9 A rectangular fish tank measures 55 centimeters by 24 centimeters by 22 centimeters. It contains 6.75 liters of water. How much water is needed to fill the tank? Give your answer in liters and milliliters. (1 L = 1,000 cm³)

10 A rectangular tank with a square base of side 60 centimeters and a height of 45 centimeters is $\frac{1}{3}$ filled with water. Water from a tap flows into the tank at 6 liters per minute. How long will it take to fill the tank completely?
(1 L = 1,000 cm³)

11 A rectangular tank, 27 centimeters by 20 centimeters by 37 centimeters, is $\frac{1}{2}$ filled with water. The water is poured into a cubical tank with an edge length of 16 centimeters until it is $\frac{3}{4}$ full. How much water is left in the rectangular tank? Give your answer in liters rounded to one decimal place.
(1 L = 1,000 cm³)

4 Real-World Problems: Volume of Composite Solids

Learning Objectives:
- Find the volume of a solid figure composed of two rectangular prisms.
- Solve real-world problems on the volume of a composite solid.

New Vocabulary
composite solid

THINK

The figure shows a large solid cube that has a small cube removed from one of its faces. The volume of the figure is 189 cubic centimeters. Given that the edge length of each cube is a whole number in centimeters, find the edge length of each cube.

ENGAGE

This solid is made up of two rectangular prisms. Discuss two different ways you can find the volume of the solid.

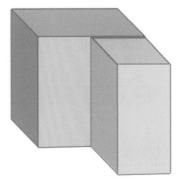

LEARN Find the volume of a solid composed of two rectangular prisms

1 Solids that are made up of two or more basic solids are called **composite solids**.
This composite solid is made up of two rectangular prisms.
Find its volume.

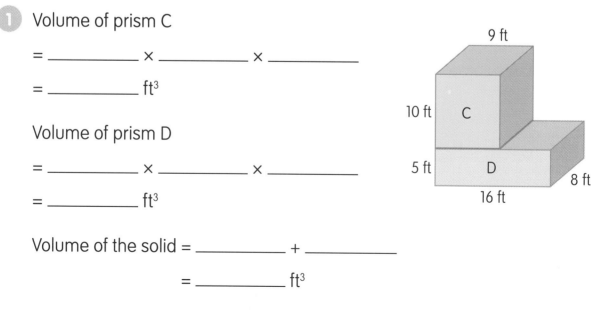

Add the volumes of the two rectangular prisms to find the volume of the solid.

Length of prism A = 4 cm
Width of prism A = 3 cm
Height of prism A = 5 cm
Volume of prism A = 4 × 3 × 5
          = 60 cm³

Length of prism B = 5 cm
Width of prism B = 3 cm
Height of prism B = 2 cm
Volume of prism B = 5 × 3 × 2
          = 30 cm³

Volume of the solid = 60 + 30 = 90 cm³

TRY Practice finding the volume of a solid composed of two rectangular prisms

Find the volume of each solid.

1 Volume of prism C

= _____ × _____ × _____

= _____ ft³

Volume of prism D

= _____ × _____ × _____

= _____ ft³

Volume of the solid = _____ + _____

          = _____ ft³

2 Volume of the prism E

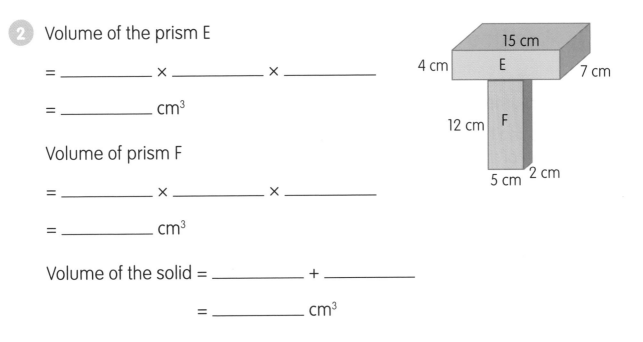

= _____ × _____ × _____

= _____ cm³

Volume of prism F

= _____ × _____ × _____

= _____ cm³

Volume of the solid = _____ + _____

= _____ cm³

ENGAGE

A box measures 24 centimeters by 16 centimeters by 27 centimeters. What is the maximum number of books that can be put into the box if each book measures 12 centimeters by 8 centimeters by 3 centimeters? Explain your method to your partner.

LEARN Find the volume of solid figures to solve real-world problems

1 Katelyn buys a pet stairs for her cat. The stairs are made up of two rectangular wooden blocks. Find the volume of the pet stairs.

Total volume of the two rectangular blocks
= (8 × 18 × 12) + (9 × 18 × 7)
= 1,728 + 1,134
= 2,862 in³

The volume of the pet stairs is 2,862 cubic inches.

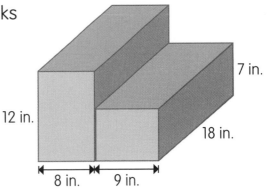

Find the volume of each solid.

1 A wooden bed frame is made up of two rectangular prisms. Find the total volume of the bed frame.

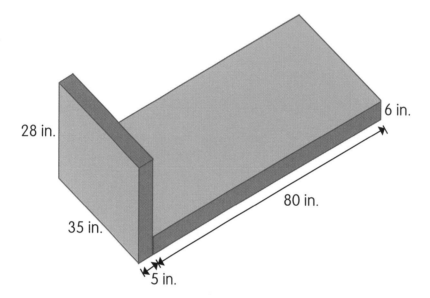

28 in.

6 in.

80 in.

35 in.

5 in.

Total volume of the bed frame

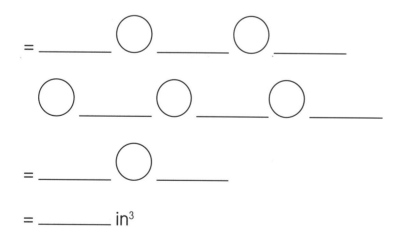

= _____ $\bigcirc$ _____ $\bigcirc$ _____

$\bigcirc$ _____ $\bigcirc$ _____ $\bigcirc$ _____

= _____ $\bigcirc$ _____

= _____ in^3

INDEPENDENT PRACTICE

Find the volume of each solid.

1

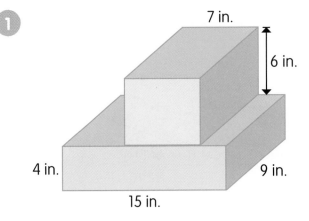

7 in.

6 in.

4 in.

9 in.

15 in.

2

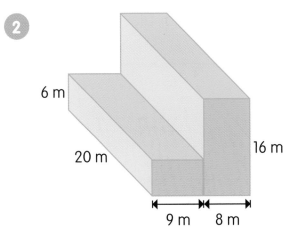

6 m

20 m

16 m

9 m   8 m

Solve.

3 An iron girder is composed of two rectangular prisms.
Find the volume of the girder.

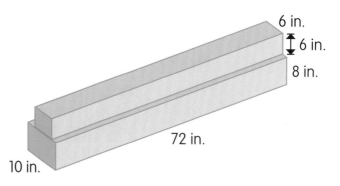

4 A cube of edge 5 centimeters is cut from a rectangular block of wood as shown. Find the volume of the remaining block.

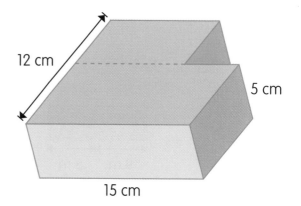

Mathematical Habit 6 Use precise mathematical language

Describe how you would find the difference between the volumes of the two prisms below.

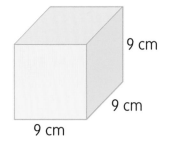

9 cm

9 cm

9 cm

Rectangular prism A

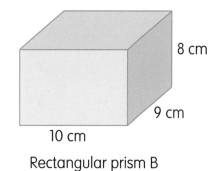

8 cm

9 cm

10 cm

Rectangular prism B

Problem Solving with Heuristics

1 **Mathematical Habit 8** **Look for patterns**

These rectangular prisms are built using 4 and 6 one-centimeter cubes.

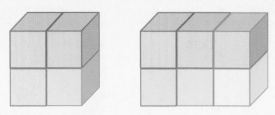

a How many different rectangular prisms can you build using 5, 6, 7, 8,

and 9 one-centimeter cubes? _____

b List the length, width, and height of each rectangular prism you have built in the table.

Number of cubes	Length (cm)	Width (cm)	Height (cm)

2 **Mathematical Habit 8** Look for patterns

Look at the pattern of staircases formed using unit cubes.

Staircase 1

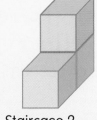
Staircase 2

Staircase 3

a Build staircases 4 and 5 using unit cubes.
Record your answer in the table.

Staircase	Number of unit cubes
1	1
2	1 + 2 = 3
3	1 + 2 + 3 = 6
4	
5	

b Without building Staircase 6, find the number of unit cubes it would take to build it.

c Find the number of unit cubes in Staircase 8.

d If each unit cube has an edge length of 1 centimeter, what are the volumes of staircases 9 and 10?

3 **Mathematical Habit 3** Construct viable arguments

The diagram shows a rectangular prism. The areas of the faces are 6 square centimeters, 10 square centimeters, and 15 square centimeters. What is the volume of the rectangular prism?

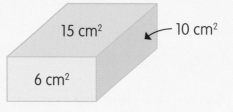

Mathematical Habit 7 Make use of structure

What is the least number of unit cubes that must be added to the figure below to form a cube?

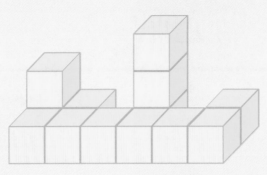

CHAPTER WRAP-UP

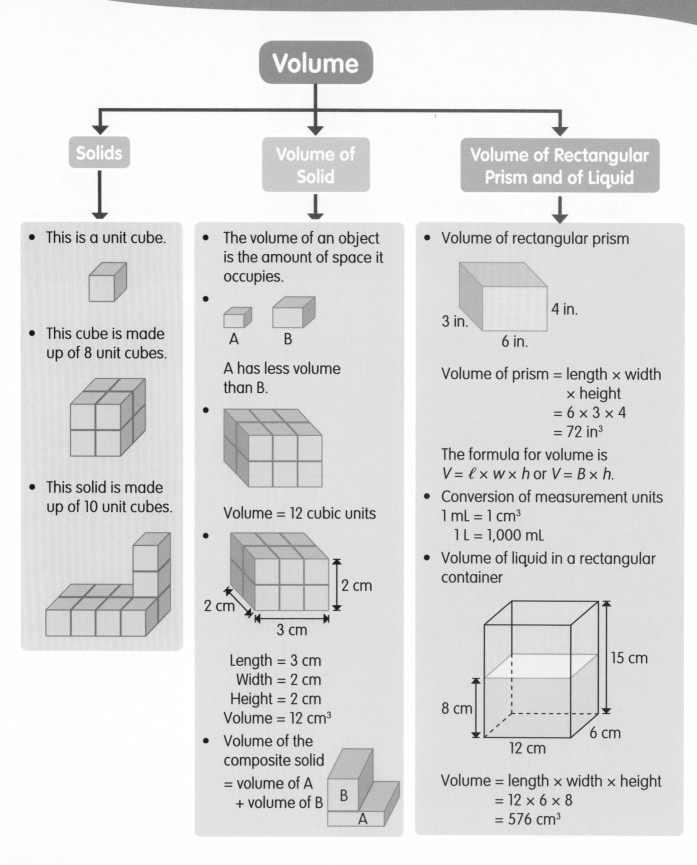

Volume

Solids

- This is a unit cube.

- This cube is made up of 8 unit cubes.

- This solid is made up of 10 unit cubes.

Volume of Solid

- The volume of an object is the amount of space it occupies.

- A B

  A has less volume than B.

- Volume = 12 cubic units

- 2 cm
  2 cm
  3 cm

  Length = 3 cm
  Width = 2 cm
  Height = 2 cm
  Volume = 12 cm³

- Volume of the composite solid
  = volume of A
  + volume of B

  B A

Volume of Rectangular Prism and of Liquid

- Volume of rectangular prism

  3 in. 4 in. 6 in.

  Volume of prism = length × width
  × height
  = 6 × 3 × 4
  = 72 in³

  The formula for volume is
  $V = \ell \times w \times h$ or $V = B \times h$.

- Conversion of measurement units
  1 mL = 1 cm³
  1 L = 1,000 mL

- Volume of liquid in a rectangular container

  15 cm
  8 cm
  12 cm
  6 cm

  Volume = length × width × height
  = 12 × 6 × 8
  = 576 cm³

Each solid is made up of unit cubes. Find the volume of each solid.

1

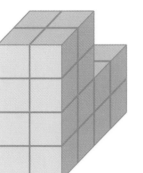

Volume = _____ cubic units

2

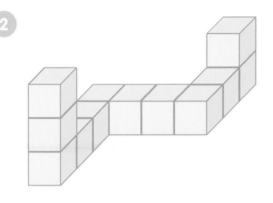

Volume = _____ cubic units

Find the volume of each solid, then compare their volumes.

3

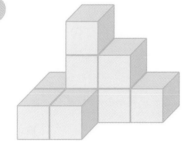   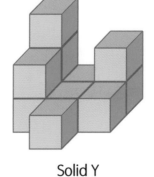

Solid X   Solid Y

Volume of Solid X = _____ cubic units

Volume of Solid Y = _____ cubic units

Solid _____ has a greater volume.

CHAPTER REVIEW

Find the volume of each rectangular prism.

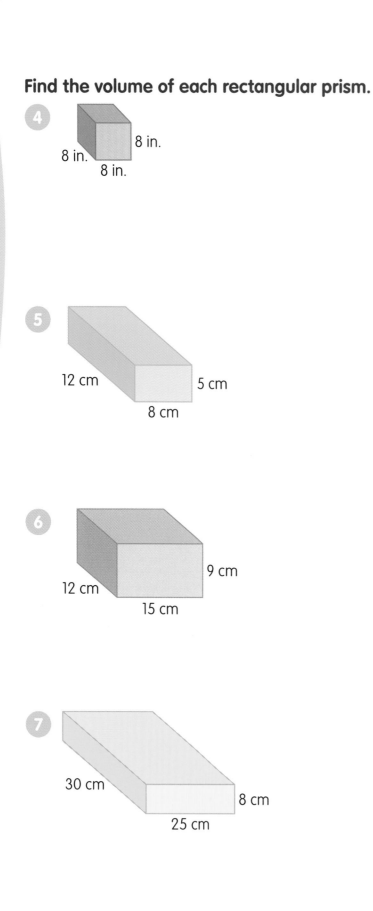

4

8 in.

8 in.

8 in.

5

12 cm

5 cm

8 cm

6

9 cm

12 cm

15 cm

7

30 cm

8 cm

25 cm

Fill in each blank.

8 5,007 mL = _____ L _____ mL

9 2 L 3 mL = _____ mL

10 375 mL = _____ cm³

11 8,129 cm³ = _____ L _____ mL

Find the volume of water in each rectangular container.

12

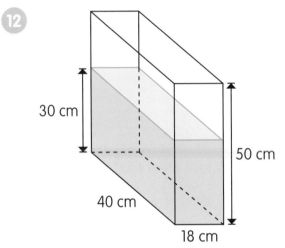

30 cm

40 cm

18 cm

50 cm

13

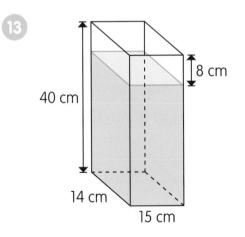

40 cm

8 cm

14 cm

15 cm

Solve.

14 Find the volume of a cube with edge length of 6 meters.

15 Find the volume of a rectangular prism measuring 12 centimeters by 7 centimeters by 9 centimeters.

16 A rectangular container measures 8 feet by 6 feet by 4 feet. Find its volume.

17 The tank is completely filled with water. If $\frac{2}{5}$ of the water from the tank is poured into another container, how much water is left in the tank?

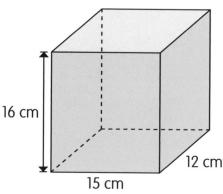

16 cm

12 cm

15 cm

18 A rectangular tank measuring 25 centimeters by 14 centimeters by 13 centimeters is filled to the brim with water. 0.78 liters of water from the tank is used up. How much water is left in the tank? Give your answer in milliliters.

19 A rectangular fish tank measures 48 centimeters by 24 centimeters by 30 centimeters. It contains 12.4 liters of water. How much more water is needed to fill the tank completely? Give your answer in liters.

20 Jessica poured water into the rectangular tank until it was $\frac{2}{3}$ full. Then, she poured some of the water out until it was $\frac{2}{5}$ full. How much water did she pour out of the tank? Give your answer in milliliters.

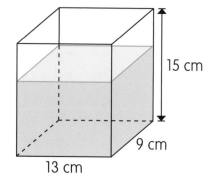

15 cm

9 cm

13 cm

21 A rectangular tank is 27 centimeters long, 18 centimeters wide, and 39 centimeters high. It is half filled with water. The water is poured into a cubical tank with edge length of 15 centimeters until it is $\frac{2}{3}$ full. How much water is left in the rectangular tank? Give your answer in liters.

22 Jason has a block of clay that is made up of two rectangular pieces of different colors. Find the volume of the block of clay.

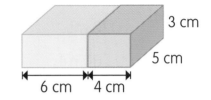

3 cm

5 cm

6 cm   4 cm

23 An aquarium is made up of two rectangular tanks with square bases. The side of each square base is 8 inches long and the heights of the two tanks are 18 inches and 12 inches. Find the capacity of the aquarium.

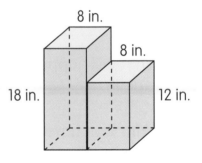

8 in.

8 in.

18 in.

12 in.

Assessment Prep

Answer each question.

24 What is the volume of the rectangular prism in cubic units?

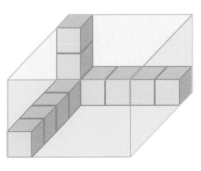

Volume of the rectangular prism = _____ cubic units

25 What is 10.2 liters in milliliters?

(A) 0.102 mL

(B) 1,020 mL

(C) 10,200 mL

(D) 102,000 mL

26 The heights of Tank A and Tank B are equal. Tank A is completely filled with water.

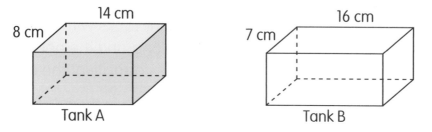

Tank A

Tank B

What will happen when all the water from Tank A is poured into Tank B? Explain.

Write your answers and explanation in the space below.

Name: _____ Date: _____

Moving to a New House

1 Brianna and her family are moving. They are trying to find a box with the **largest** volume to pack their clothes.

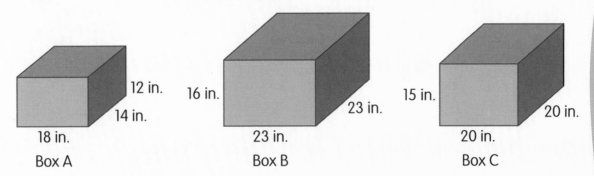

12 in.

14 in.

18 in.

Box A

16 in.

23 in.

23 in.

Box B

15 in.

20 in.

20 in.

Box C

Which box should they choose? Explain your answer.

2 Brianna stumbles upon some 3-inch cube-shaped wooden blocks and decides to glue them together to form the solid as shown below. What is the volume of the solid?

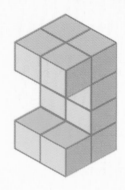

3 After moving, Brianna buys a rectangular fish tank measuring 50 centimeters by 15 centimeters by 20 centimeters. She fills it with 6.75 liters of water. What is the height of the water level in the tank? How many more liters of water is needed to fill the tank completely?

Rubric

Point(s)	Level	My Performance
7–8	4	• Most of my answers are correct. • I showed complete understanding of what I have learned. • I used the correct strategies to solve the problems. • I explained my answers and mathematical thinking clearly and completely.
5–6	3	• Some of my answers are correct. • I showed some understanding of what I have learned. • I used some correct strategies to solve the problems. • I explained my answers and mathematical thinking clearly.
3–4	2	• A few of my answers are correct. • I showed little understanding of what I have learned. • I used a few correct strategies to solve the problems. • I explained some of my answers and mathematical thinking clearly.
0–2	1	• A few of my answers are correct. • I showed little or no understanding of what I have learned. • I used a few strategies to solve the problems. • I did not explain my answers and mathematical thinking clearly.

Teacher's Comments

STEAM

Op Art

The word *optical* is related to seeing. An optical illusion [ih-LEW-zhun] is a picture that fools your eyes. Some artists use colors, shapes, and patterns to make art that seems to move. These optical illusions are examples of op art.

Task

Build an Op Art Mobile

Work in pairs or small groups to make op art mobiles.

1. Collect papers, pencils, markers, scissors, a ruler, a roll of adhesive tape, a coat hanger, and a spool of thread.

2. Go online to find a pattern for making a paper cube. Use the pattern as a model.

3. Use the model to draw a set of patterns for 5 or more cubes of different volumes. Calculate the total volume.

4. Cut a long piece of thread for each cube. Put the pieces of thread aside for later use.

5. Go to the library or go online to find examples of op art. You might want to look for work by the artists Bridget Riley, Victor Vasarely, and Frank Stella.

6. Decorate each cube pattern with op art. Cut out each pattern and leave it flat. Place the end of one piece of thread inside one corner where two sides meet. Tape the piece of thread in place. Then, fold each pattern and seal the edges to make cubes.

7. Hang the cubes from the bottom of the coat hanger. Cut the pieces of thread to change the heights of the cubes.

8. Hang the op-art mobiles. Discuss the optical illusions you see. Compare and graph total volumes.

Line Plots and the Coordinate Plane

How can we represent the growth of these plants in graphs?

How can we represent data in line plots? How can you describe a point on a coordinate plane? How can you use the coordinate plane to show number patterns?

Name: _____ Date: _____

Making and interpreting a line plot

You can make a line plot to show the frequency of data on a number line. The data may be recorded in a table, a tally chart, or another form.

The tally chart shows the height of each plant grown from seed in three months.

Height of Plant (ft)	Tally
0	|
$\frac{1}{2}$	||
$\frac{3}{4}$	||||
1	|||
$1\frac{1}{2}$	|

The data can be represented in a line plot as shown.
Each ✗ represents 1 plant.

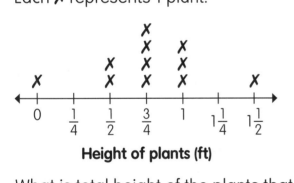

Height of plants (ft)

What is total height of the plants that are between 0 and 1 foot tall?

$$\frac{1}{2} + \frac{1}{2} + \frac{3}{4} + \frac{3}{4} + \frac{3}{4} + \frac{3}{4} = 4$$

The total height of the plants that are between 0 and 1 foot tall is 4 feet.

▶ **Quick Check**

The tally chart shows the weight of a potato in each bag.

Weight of Potato (oz)	Tally
$1\frac{1}{2}$	|
$2\frac{1}{2}$	||
$3\frac{1}{2}$	ЖHT
$4\frac{1}{2}$	|||
$5\frac{1}{2}$	||||

Use the data to draw a line plot.

1

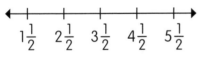

Weight of potatoes (oz)

Use the line plot to answer **2** **and** **3**.

2 How many potatoes are there in all?

3 What is the least possible weight of three potatoes?

Making and interpreting a line graph

You can draw a line graph to show how data changes over time.
The data may be recorded in a table, a tally chart, or another form.

The table shows the temperature at different times of the day in a city.

Time	7 A.M.	8 A.M.	9 A.M.	10 A.M.	11 A.M.	12 P.M.
Temperature (°F)	60	63	67	69	73	75

The data can be represented in a line graph as shown.

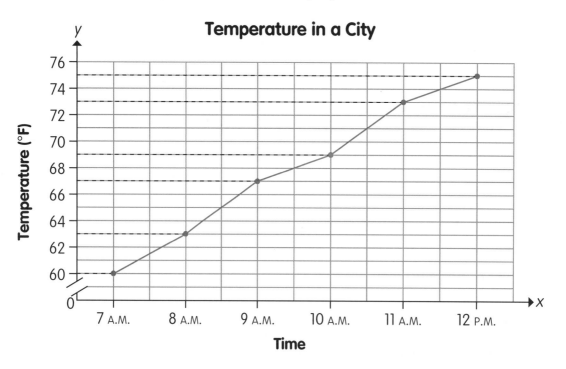

a What was the difference in temperature between 9 A.M. and 10 A.M.?
   The difference was 2 degrees Fahrenheit.

b What was the highest temperature recorded?
   The highest temperature recorded was 75 degrees Fahrenheit.

c At what time was the temperature 73 degrees Fahrenheit recorded?
   The time was 11 A.M.

▶ Quick Check

The table shows the growth in height of a boy in 8 years.

Age (years)	0	2	4	6	8
Height (cm)	50	85	105	115	130

Use the data to draw a line graph.

4

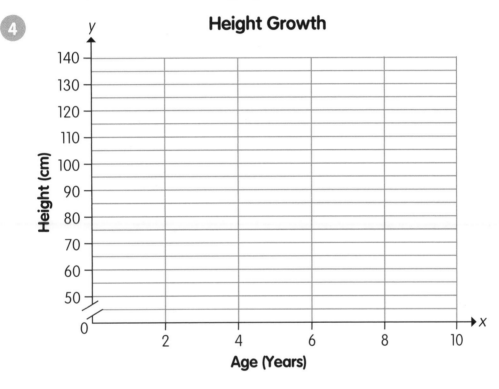

Height Growth

Age (Years)

Use the line graph to answer 5 to 7.

5 How tall was the boy when he was 6 years old?

6 How old was the boy when he was 105 centimeters tall?

7 When did the greatest increase in height occur?

Four operations involving fractions

a $\quad 1\frac{3}{4} + 2\frac{1}{5} = 3\frac{15}{20} + \frac{4}{20}$

$\qquad\qquad = 3\frac{19}{20}$

b $\quad 3\frac{2}{3} - 1\frac{6}{7} = 2\frac{14}{21} - \frac{18}{21}$

$\qquad\qquad = 1\frac{35}{21} - \frac{18}{21}$

$\qquad\qquad = 1\frac{17}{21}$

c $\quad \frac{5}{6} \times 24 = \frac{5 \times \overset{4}{\cancel{24}}}{\underset{1}{\cancel{6}}}$

$\qquad\qquad = 20$

▶ Quick Check

Solve.

8 $\frac{3}{5} + \frac{1}{4}$

9 $\frac{2}{3} + \frac{3}{8}$

10 $3\frac{5}{6} + 2\frac{4}{9}$

11 $\frac{9}{10} - \frac{2}{5}$

12 $7\frac{1}{3} - 3\frac{6}{7}$

13 $8 - 6\frac{4}{5}$

14 $12 \times \frac{3}{5}$

15 $1\frac{1}{8} \times 4$

1 Making and Interpreting Line Plots

Learning Objectives:
- Make and interpret line plots with fractional data.
- Use fractions and their operations to solve problems using data.

THINK

Landon drew a line plot to show different volumes of water in some bottles.
He missed out two bottles in his line plot.

a Is it possible to have the least number of $1\frac{1}{2}$-liter bottles? Explain.

b If the total volume of water was $20\frac{1}{2}$ liters, what would be the volume of the two missing bottles. Explain and show your answer.

Each **✗** represents 1 bottle.

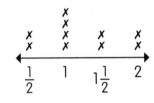

Volume of water in liters

ENGAGE

Measure each piece of ribbon in inches.

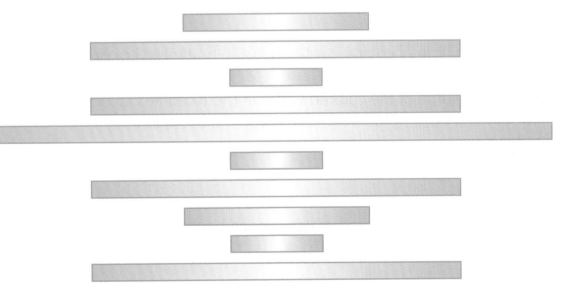

Now, record the length of each piece of ribbon in feet. Then, create a data display. Share with your partner how you did it.

LEARN Make and interpret line plots

1 Emma carried out a science experiment. She measured the volumes of colored water in 10 identical bottles and recorded her data in a table.

Volume (qt)	$\frac{1}{8}$	$\frac{1}{4}$	$\frac{3}{8}$	$\frac{1}{2}$
Number of Bottles	2	4	2	2

Emma then made a line plot to show the results of her experiment. Each ✗ represents 1 bottle.

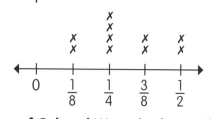

$\frac{2}{8} = \frac{1}{4}$ and $\frac{4}{8} = \frac{1}{2}$.

Volume of Colored Water in the Bottles (qt)

a What is the total volume of colored water in the 10 bottles?

$$\text{Total volume} = \left(2 \times \frac{1}{8}\right) + \left(4 \times \frac{1}{4}\right) + \left(2 \times \frac{3}{8}\right) + \left(2 \times \frac{1}{2}\right)$$

$$= \frac{1}{4} + 1 + \frac{3}{4} + 1$$

$$= 3 \text{ qt}$$

The total volume of colored water in the 10 bottles is 3 quarts.

b The total volume of the colored water in the 10 bottles is redistributed equally into each bottle. What is the volume of colored water in each bottle now?

$$3 \div 10 = \frac{3}{10}$$

The total volume of colored water in each bottle is now $\frac{3}{10}$ quart.

TRY Practice making and interpreting line plots

The tally chart shows the weights of the raisins in 12 bags of trail mix.

Weight of Raisins (oz)	Number of Bags
$\frac{1}{2}$		
$\frac{3}{4}$	||
1			
$1\frac{1}{4}$	|||
$1\frac{1}{2}$		
$1\frac{3}{4}$		
2			

Use the data to fill in the table and make a line plot.

1 Table:

Weight of Raisins (oz)							
Number of Bags							

Line plot:

Each ✗ represent 1 bag.

Weights of raisins in bags (oz)

Use the line plot in ① to answer ② and ③.

② What is the total weight of the raisins in the 12 bags?

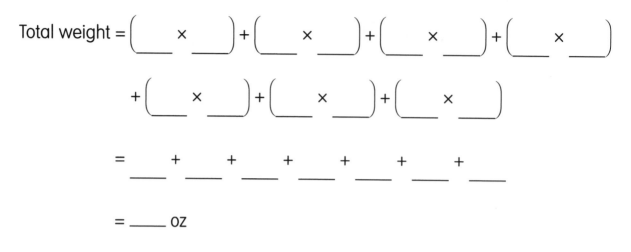

The total weight of the raisins in the 12 bags is _____ ounces.

③ If these raisins were distributed equally among the 12 bags, what would be the weight of the raisins in each bag?

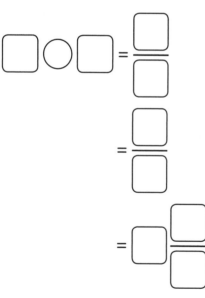

The weight of the raisins in each bag is _____ ounces.

INDEPENDENT PRACTICE

The table shows the weights of 10 wedges of cheese.

Weight (lb)	$\frac{1}{8}$	$\frac{1}{4}$	$\frac{3}{8}$	$\frac{1}{2}$
Number of Wedges	3	3	1	3

Use the data to make line plot.

1

Use the line plot in ① to answer ② and ③.

2 What is the total weight of the 10 wedges of cheese?

3 All 10 wedges of cheese are used to create 10 cheese platters of identical weight. What is the weight of the cheese on each platter?

The table shows the lengths of 15 sticks of clay.

Length (ft)	$\frac{1}{10}$	$\frac{1}{5}$	$\frac{3}{10}$	$\frac{2}{5}$	$\frac{1}{2}$
Number of Sticks	2	4	1	3	5

Use the data to make line plot.

4

Use the line plot in 4 to answer questions 5 to 7.

5 What is the total length of the 15 sticks of clay?

6 The sticks of clay are joined together from end to end. Then, they are divided into 15 sticks of equal length. What is the length of each new stick of clay?

7 Predict what the line plot for the new sticks of clay in 6 would look like. Do not draw the line plot.

2 Graphing on a Coordinate Plane

Learning Objectives:
- Read points on a coordinate plane.
- Plot points on a coordinate plane.
- Use ordered pairs to draw line graphs.

New Vocabulary
coordinate plane	*x*-axis
y-axis	coordinates
ordered pair	origin
x-coordinate	*y*-coordinate

THINK

Mīa started walking at point P. Each step she took was in the direction of north, south, east, or west. She returned to point P after 10 steps. Use grid paper to sketch four different paths she could take.

ENGAGE

20 desks are arranged in rows and columns in a classroom.

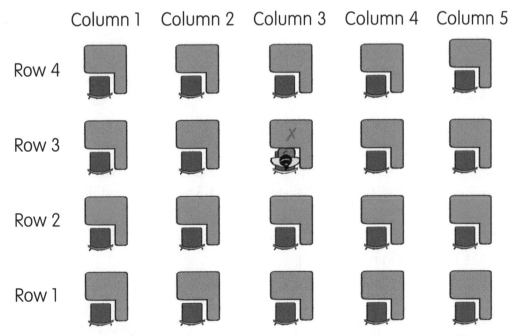

Sally is sitting at the desk marked ✗. How do you describe the position of her desk? Choose another desk and describe its position to your partner.

LEARN Read and plot points on the coordinate plane

1 You can use a coordinate plane to locate points in a plane. A coordinate plane has a horizontal number line and a vertical number line.

> The horizontal number line is called the *x*-axis and the vertical number line is called the *y*-axis.

These axes are number lines, so they are marked with numbers. You can name or locate any point on this coordinate plane with two numbers, called coordinates.

This coordinate plane is marked with two points, A (2, 5) and B (4, 3).

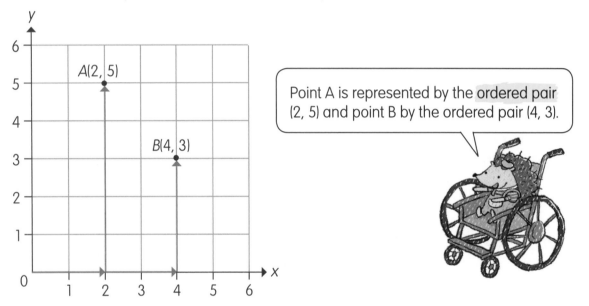

> Point A is represented by the ordered pair (2, 5) and point B by the ordered pair (4, 3).

The point A is 2 units to the right of the *y*-axis and 5 units above the *x*-axis. The point B is 4 units to the right of the *y*-axis and 3 units above the *x*-axis.

The point at which the *x*-axis and the *y*-axis intersect is called the origin. The coordinates of the origin are (0, 0).

> The *x*-coordinate is always named first and the *y*-coordinate second. A (1,6) means 1 is the *x*-coordinate and 6 is the *y*-coordinate of the point A.

© 2020 Marshall Cavendish Education Pte Ltd

TRY Practice reading and plotting points on the coordinate plane

Use the coordinate plane to answer ① to ⑥.

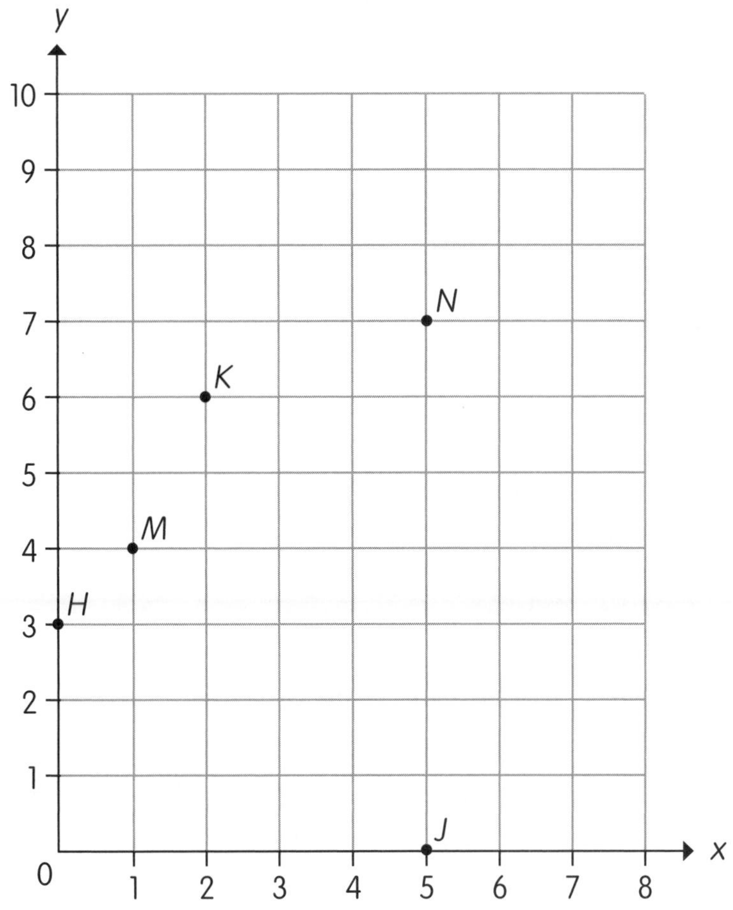

(coordinate plane graph with points plotted: N at (5, 7), K at (2, 6), M at (1, 4), H at (0, 3), J at (5, 0))

① Plot the points P (3, 6), Q (4, 5), and R (4, 8).

② Coordinates of H = _____

③ Coordinates of J = _____

④ Coordinates of K = _____

⑤ Coordinates of M = _____

⑥ Coordinates of N = _____

Use the coordinate plane to answer 7 to 12.

The coordinate plane shows the map of part of New York City.

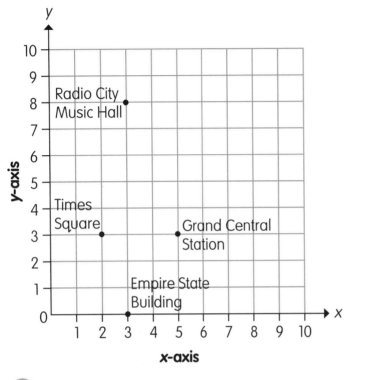

7   What is the ordered pair representing the Empire State Building? _____

8   Jacob is at Grand Central Station. What are the coordinates for his location?

    _____

9   Ava is 5 units to the right of Radio City Music Hall. What is the ordered pair
    of her location? _____

10 The Carnegie Hall is 1 unit to the left and 2 units above the Radio City
    Music Hall. Draw the location of Carnegie Hall on the coordinate plane.

11 The Museum of Modern Art is 2 units to the right and 1 unit above the
    Radio City Music Hall. Draw the location of Museum of Modern Art on the
    coordinate plane.

12 Emilia describes the ordered pair of Times Square as (3, 2). Is she correct?
    Explain.

    _____

    _____

James is playing a game. He needs to place three dots in a diagonal line on the coordinate plane. What are some possible placements? What happens if he connects the dots? Share your thinking with your partner.

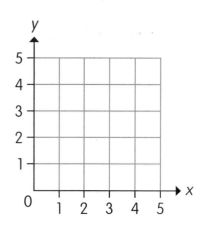

LEARN Graph on the coordinate plane

1. Alexis buys some granola bars from a supermarket. Each granola bar costs $2. The table shows the total cost of the granola bars.

Number of Granola Bars	1	2	3	4	5
Total Cost ($)	2	4	6	8	10

Alexis uses the data in the table to plot the ordered pairs (1, 2), (2, 4), (3, 6), (4, 8), and (5, 10) in a coordinate plane. The x-axis shows the number of granola bars. The y-axis shows the total cost of the granola bars.

Alexis joins the points in the coordinate plane using a straight line. This line is called a line graph.

From the graph, you can find the x-coordinate if the y-coordinate is known and vice versa.

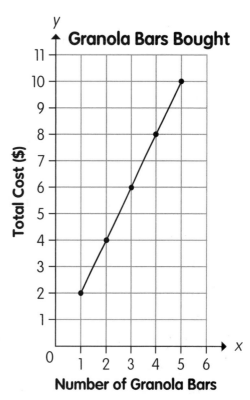

Granola Bars Bought

2 The table shows the amount of snowfall over several days.

Day	1	2	3	4	5
Snow Level (in.)	5	6	7	10	15

The data in the table can also be shown in a line graph.

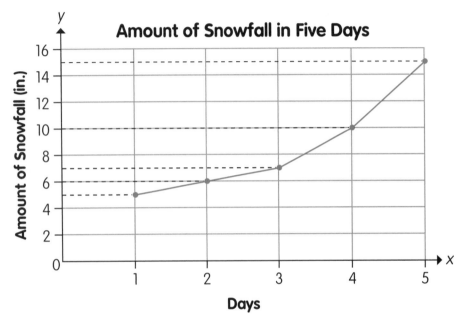

a What is the total amount of snowfall in the five days?

5 + 6 + 7 + 10 + 15 = 43

The total amount of snowfall in the five days is 43 inches.

b What was the greatest amount of snowfall recorded? When was it recorded?

The greatest amount of snowfall recorded was 15 inches. It was recorded on Day 5.

c Between which two days was the increase in the amount of snowfall the greatest? How much was the increase?

To find the greatest increase, look for the interval with the greatest increase in the y-axis. The greatest increase in the amount of snowfall was between Days 4 and 5. The increase was 5 inches.

TRY Practice graphing on the coordinate plane

The table shows Jade's height from 0 to 5 years old.

Year	0	1	2	3	4	5
Height (cm)	50	75	90	100	105	115

**Use the data in the table to make a line graph and label the axes.
Use intervals of 10 on the vertical scale.**

1

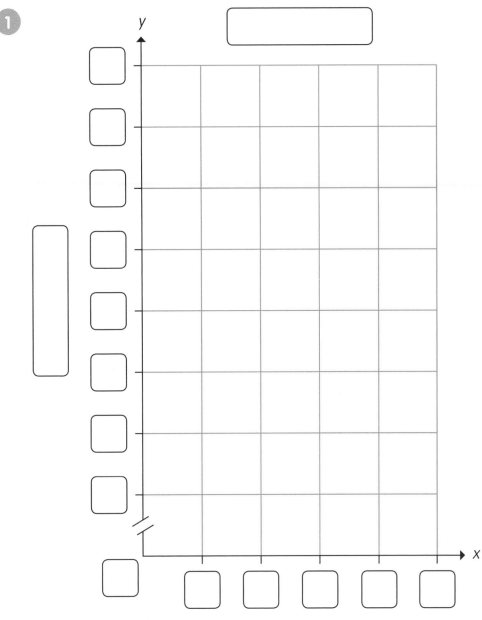

Use the data in the graph to answer questions ② to ⑥.

The graph shows the cost of fabric measured in yards.

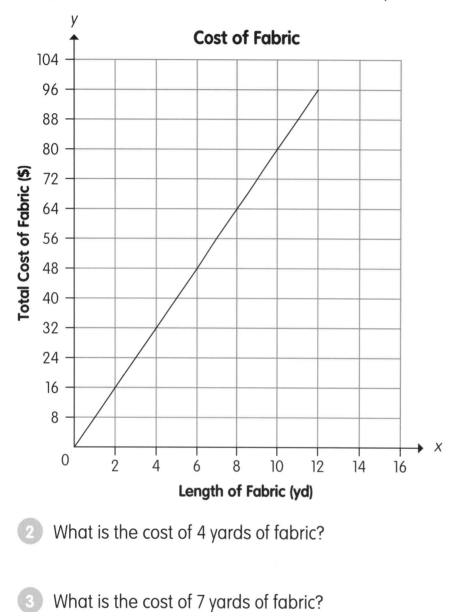

② What is the cost of 4 yards of fabric?

③ What is the cost of 7 yards of fabric?

④ What is the cost of 11 yards of fabric?

⑤ How many yards of fabric can you buy with $40?

⑥ How many yards of fabric can you buy with $72?

The table shows the weight of a kitten from 0 to 7 weeks old.

Week	0	1	2	3	4	5	6	7
Weight (oz)	4	8	12	16	18	22	26	32

Use the data in the table to make a line graph and label the axes. Use intervals of 4 on the vertical scale.

7

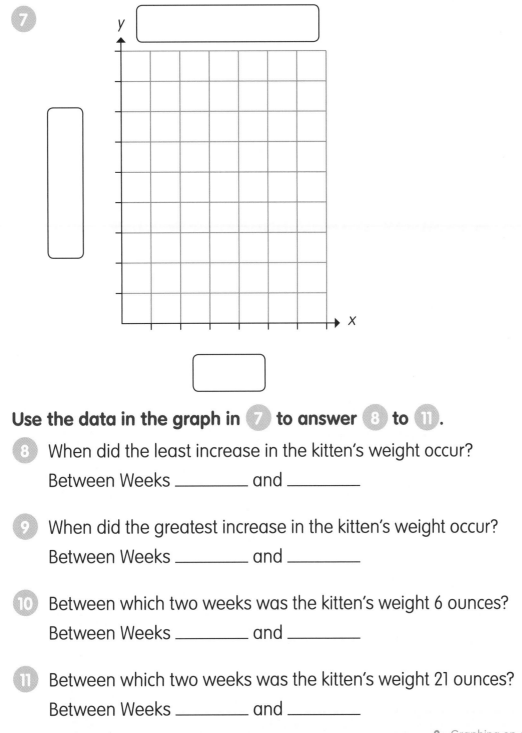

Use the data in the graph in 7 to answer 8 to 11.

8 When did the least increase in the kitten's weight occur?

Between Weeks _____ and _____

9 When did the greatest increase in the kitten's weight occur?

Between Weeks _____ and _____

10 Between which two weeks was the kitten's weight 6 ounces?

Between Weeks _____ and _____

11 Between which two weeks was the kitten's weight 21 ounces?

Between Weeks _____ and _____

Name: _____   Date: _____

BATTLESHIP WARS

What you need:

Players: 2
Materials: 10 × 10 coordinate grids

What to do:

1 Each player receives 2 coordinate grids, label the x and y axes 1 through 10. Then, label one "Self" and the other "Opponent". Arrange the following ships on the grid labeled "Self".

Ships	Space it occupies on the grid
Aircraft carrier	5
Battleship	4
Submarine	3
Cruiser	3
Destroyer	2

The ships must be placed horizontally or vertically. Do not place the ships diagonally. Do not allow the other player to look at your grid.

2 Player 1 calls out a location on the grid. If a ship is found at the location, Player 2 says "Hit!" Otherwise, he or she says "Missed!" Player 1 uses the "Opponent" grid to record each location called out by shading it for a hit or drawing a cross for a miss. Player 2 does the same on the "Self" grid.

3 Take turns to try to sink each other's ships. A ship is sunk when all the spaces it occupies on the grid have been called out. The player whose ship is sunk says "My ship is sunk!"

4 The player who sinks all his or her opponent's ships wins.

INDEPENDENT PRACTICE

Write down the coordinates of each point on the coordinate plane.

1 Coordinates of W = _____

2 Coordinates of X = _____

3 Coordinates of Y = _____

4 Coordinates of Z = _____

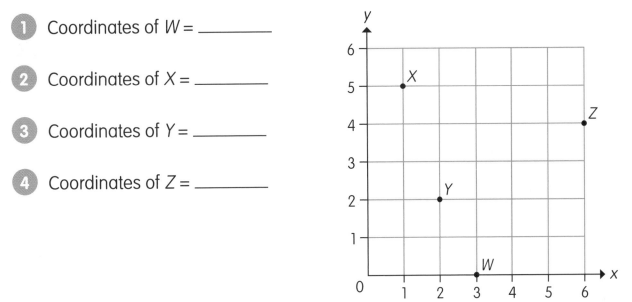

Plot each point on the coordinate plane.

5 Point A (2, 3)

6 Point B (4, 5)

7 Point C (0, 7)

8 Point D (3, 8)

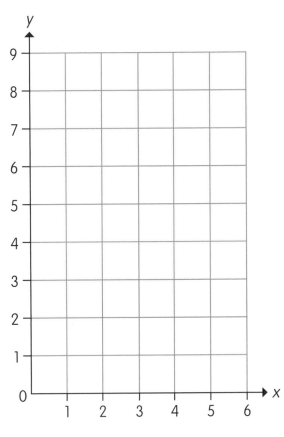

Use the data in the line graph to answer 9 to 12.

The graph shows the cost of ribbons measured in yards.

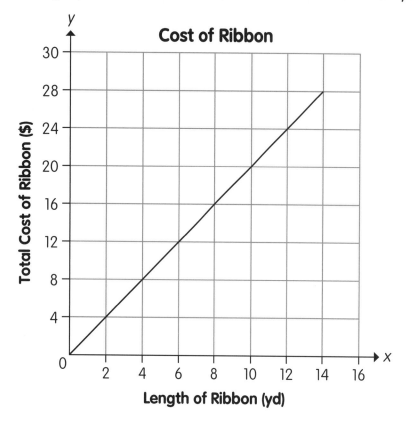

9 What is the cost of 8 yards of ribbon?

10 What is the cost of 11 yards of ribbon?

11 How many yards of ribbons can you buy with $8?

12 How many yards of ribbons can you buy with $26?

 3 Number Patterns and Graphs

Learning Objectives:
- Identify and extend number patterns.
- Identify the relationship between two sets of numbers.

> **New Vocabulary**
> term

THINK

Mr. Taylor earns $50 for every hour he works. Ms. Martin earns $80 for every hour she works. On a weekday, Mr. Taylor starts work 3 hours earlier than Ms. Martin. How many hours does Ms. Martin need to work to earn the same amount of money as Mr. Taylor on the same day?

ENGAGE

1. Look at each number pattern.
   a 2, 4, 8, 16, ...
   b 2, 3, 5, 8, 13, ...

   Discuss with your partner how you can find the rule of the patterns.

2. Look at the number pattern. What is the missing number in each blank?
   ____, ____, 6, 8, 10, 12, ...

LEARN Identify and extend number patterns

1. Look at this number pattern.

   1, 3, 9, 27, ...
   The first term is 1.
   The second term is $3 = 1 \times 3$.
   The third term is $9 = 3 \times 3$.
   The fourth term is $27 = 9 \times 3$.
   The fifth term is $27 \times 3 = 81$.
   The sixth term is $81 \times 3 = 243$.

   > Multiply each term by 3 to get the next term.

   > A term in a number pattern is any number in that number pattern.

2 Here is another number pattern.

1, 3, 6, 10, 15, ...
The first term is 1.
The second term is 3 = 1 + 2.
The third term is 6 = (1 + 2) + 3.
The fourth term is 10 = (1 + 2 + 3) + 4.
The fifth term is 15 = (1 + 2 + 3 + 4) + 5.
The sixth term is 21 = (1 + 2 + 3 + 4 + 5) + 6.
The seventh term is 28 = (1 + 2 + 3 + 4 + 5 + 6) + 7.

To get the eighth term, add 8 to the seventh term.

To get the twelfth term, add 12 to the eleventh term.

3 Two sets of numbers can be related.
a Look at this table.

Rodrigo's Age (yr)	11	12	13	14	15
His Sister's Age (yr)	8	9	10	11	12

To get his sister's age, subtract 3 from Rodrigo's age.

The table shows that Rodrigo's sister is 3 years younger than him.

b Here is another table.

Length of Side of Square (cm)	1	2	3	4	5
Perimeter of Square (cm)	4	8	12	16	20

To get the perimeter, multiply the length by 4.

This table shows that the perimeter of a square is 4 times the length of its side.

4. Each week in summer, Lily buys 4 baseball cards and 2 football cards. The table shows the total number of cards she has collected after each week.

Week	1	2	3	4	5
Total number of baseball cards	4	8	12	16	20
Total number of football cards	2	4	6	8	10

The total number of baseball cards and the total number of football cards form patterns.

To find the total number of baseball cards, add 4 to each term to find the next term.

To find the total number of football cards, add 2 to each term to find the next term.

TRY Practice identifying and extending number patterns

Identify the rule in each pattern.

1. Pattern:

2	14	26	38	50	...

Rule: _____

2. Pattern:

630	615	600	585	570	...

Rule: _____

3. Pattern:

6	24	96	384	1,536	...

Rule: _____

4. Pattern:

46,656	7,776	1,296	216	36	...

Rule: _____

Use a rule to complete each pattern.

5 Each week, Mr. Flores buys 3 books and 5 magazines. The table shows the total number of books and magazines he has after each week.

Rule: Add _____

Rule: Add _____

Week	1	2	3	4	5
Number of books	3	6	9		
Number of magazines	5	10	15		

ENGAGE

A caterpillar crawls 2 centimeters in 1 minute. A millipede crawls 3 centimeters in 4 minutes. Draw two graphs to show the distance the two animals crawl in 12 minutes.

LEARN Generate patterns and draw graphs

1 Two water bottles A and B are being filled at two different taps. Bottle A is being filled at a rate of 50 milliliters of water every second. Bottle B is being filled at a rate of 25 milliliters of water every second. The tables show the total amount of water in the two water bottles during the first 5 seconds.

Water Collected in Bottle A

Time (s)	0	1	2	3	4	5
Total Volume of Water Collected (mL)	0	50	100	150	200	250

The ordered pairs that can be formed from the table are (0, 0), (1, 50), (2, 100), (3, 150), (4, 200), and (5, 250). When these points are plotted on a graph and joined, they form a straight line.

Water Collected in Bottle B

Time (s)	0	1	2	3	4	5
Total Volume of Water Collected (mL)	0	25	50	75	100	125

When the data from Bottle B are plotted on a graph and joined, they form a straight line.

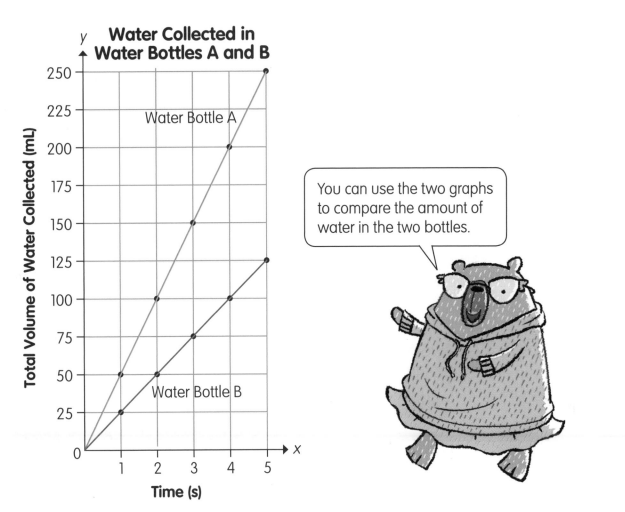

Water Collected in Water Bottles A and B

Total Volume of Water Collected (mL)

Water Bottle A

Water Bottle B

Time (s)

You can use the two graphs to compare the amount of water in the two bottles.

a How much water is in each bottle after 4 seconds?

Bottle A has 200 milliliters of water and Bottle B has 100 milliliters.

Find the grid line at 4 seconds on the horizontal axis, and see where it crosses each graph.

b Which bottle contains more water at 5 seconds? How much more?

250 − 125 = 125

Bottle A contains 125 more milliliters of water.

Find the difference between the amount of water in Bottles A and B.

c At what time do the bottles contain the same amount of water?

At 0 seconds, both have 0 milliliters of water. So, the only time the two bottles contain the same amount is before any water has been added to the bottles.

Look for a time at which the volumes are the same.

d How is the amount of water in Bottle A related to the amount of water in Bottle B at each point in time?

At each point in time, the amount of water in Bottle A is twice as much as in Bottle B.

2 Look at these two number patterns.
Pattern A: 3, 6, 9, 12, . . .
Pattern B: 4, 8, 12, 16, . . .

You can describe Pattern A as "add 3 to each term to get the next one" or "multiply each position number by 3".

You can relate the number in the pattern to its position in the number pattern.

Position Number of Term in Pattern A	1	2	3	4	5	6	7
Term	3	6	9	12	15	18	21

Position Number of Term in Pattern B	1	2	3	4	5	6	7
Term	4	8	12	16	20	24	28

You can make and graph the set of ordered pairs for Pattern A. You can do the same for Pattern B as shown on the next page. Each one should form a straight line.

© 2020 Marshall Cavendish Education Pte Ltd

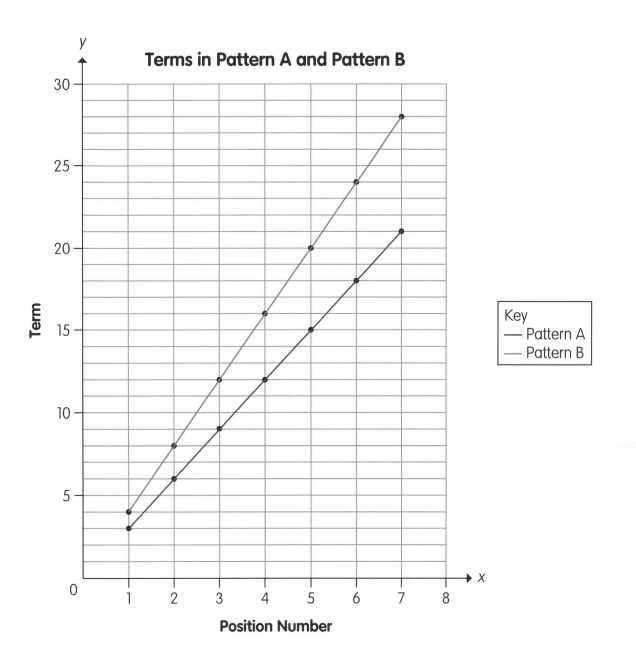

Terms in Pattern A and Pattern B

Key
— Pattern A
— Pattern B

From the graphs, each term of Pattern A is $\frac{3}{4}$ times the value of each term in the same position of Pattern B.

Practice generating patterns and drawing graphs

Complete the number pattern. Then, plot each point on a coordinate plane and make a line graph.

1 Car A consumes 1 gallon of gas for every 35 miles it travels. Car B consumes 2 gallons of gas for every 60 miles it travels.

Gas Consumed (gal)	1	2	3	4	5
Distance Car A Travels (mi)	35	70	105		

Gas Consumed (gal)	2	4	6
Distance Car B Travels (mi)	60	120	180

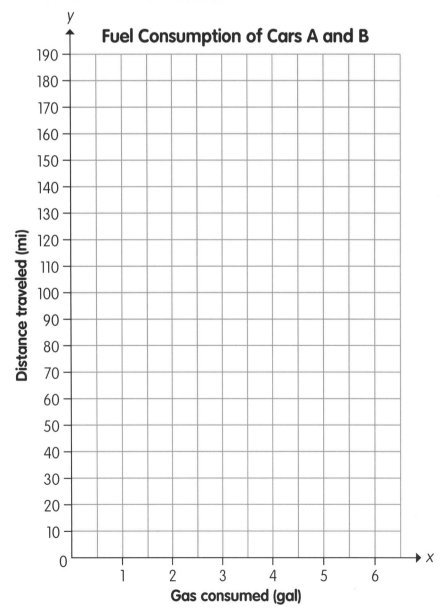

Use the data in the line graph in ➊ to answer ➋ to ➎.

➋ How far can each car travel on 3 gallons of gas?

➌ Which car travels farther on 2 gallons of gas? How much farther?

➍ How far can each car travel on 5 gallons of gas?

➎ Which car is more fuel efficient? Explain.

Use number patterns C and D to answer ⑥ **and** ⑦.

Pattern C: 6, 12, 18, 24, 30 …
Pattern D: 4, 8, 12, 16, 20 …

⑥ Graph each number pattern on the same coordinate grid.

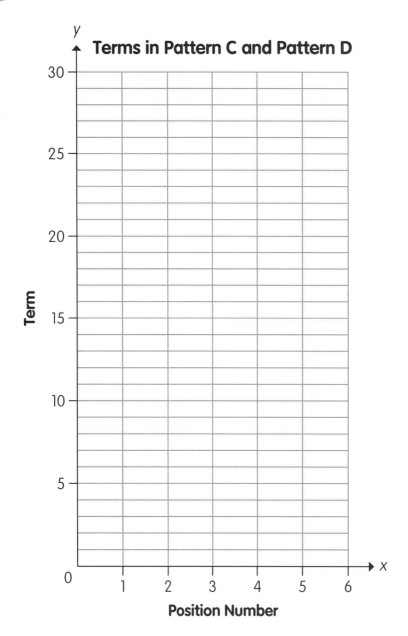

⑦ How do the terms in the same position compare to each other?

Name: _____ Date: _____

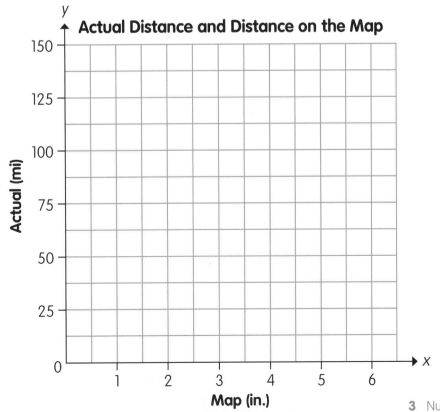

INDEPENDENT PRACTICE

Identify the rule in each pattern.

1 Pattern:

9	12	15	18	21	...

Rule: _____

2 Pattern:

26	52	104	208	416	...

Rule: _____

Complete the number pattern. Then, plot each point on the coordinate plane and make a line graph.

3 Catalina is drawing a map of her neighborhood. She uses 1 inch to represent 25 miles on her map.

Map (in.)	1	2	3	4	5
Actual (mi)	25				

The distance on the map and actual distance written as ordered pairs are

_____.

Actual Distance and Distance on the Map

Use number patterns A and B to answer each question.

Pattern A: 16, 32, 48, 64 . . .
Pattern B: 12, 24, 36, 48 . . .

4 Graph each number pattern on the same coordinate grid. Use intervals of 8 on the vertical scale.

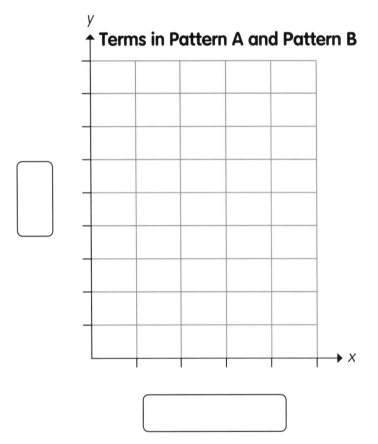

5 How do the terms in the same position compare to each other?

Mathematical Habit 5 Use tools strategically

The table shows the weights of dried apricots in 15 bags of dried fruit mixed.

Weight of dried apricot (oz)	Number of bags
$\frac{1}{2}$	|||
$\frac{3}{4}$	||||
1			
$1\frac{1}{4}$		
$1\frac{1}{2}$		
$1\frac{3}{4}$	||
2			

Draw a line plot for this information and write a question that you can ask.

Problem Solving with Heuristics

1 **Mathematical Habit 8** **Look for patterns**

Use number patterns P and Q to answer **a** to **d**. Use intervals of 2 on the vertical scale.

Pattern P: 2, 4, 6, 8, 10 …
Pattern Q: 2, 6, 10, 14, 18, …

a Graph each number pattern on the same coordinate grid.

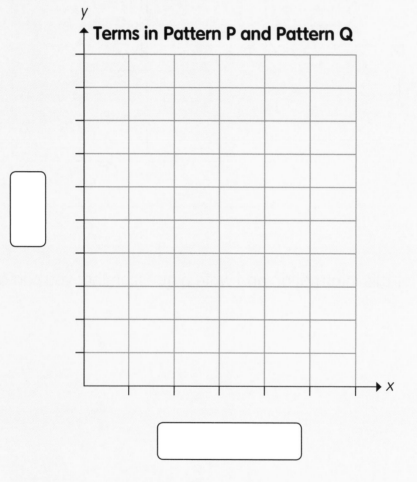

b Each term in Pattern R is twice the corresponding term in Pattern P. Find the first five terms in Pattern R.

© 2020 Marshall Cavendish Education Pte Ltd

c How do the terms in the same position of Pattern Q and Pattern R compare to each other?

d How do the terms in the same position of Pattern P and Pattern Q compare to each other?

2 **Mathematical Habit 7** **Make use of structure**

Write down a possible pair of coordinates of point C such that the points A, B, and C form

a a right triangle.

b an acute triangle.

c an obtuse triangle.

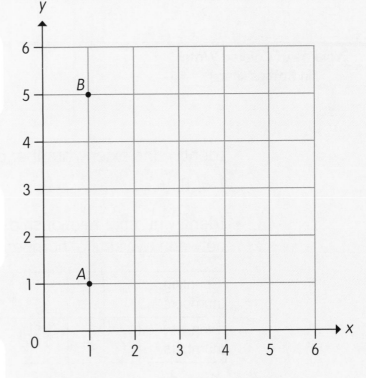

CHAPTER WRAP-UP

? How can we represent data in line plots? How can you describe a point on a coordinate plane? How can you use the coordinate plane to show number patterns?

Line Plots and the Coordinate Plane

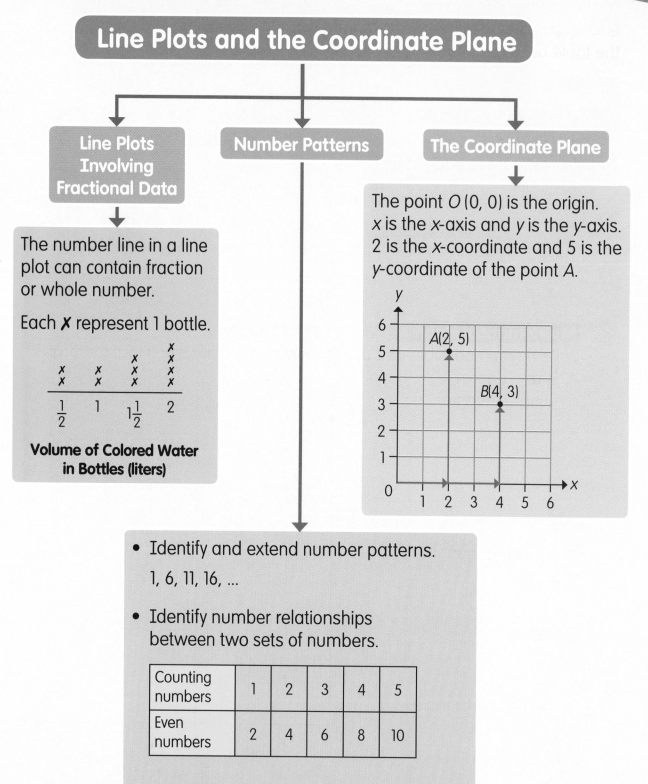

Line Plots Involving Fractional Data

The number line in a line plot can contain fraction or whole number.

Each **✗** represent 1 bottle.

Volume of Colored Water in Bottles (liters)

Number Patterns

The Coordinate Plane

The point O (0, 0) is the origin. x is the x-axis and y is the y-axis. 2 is the x-coordinate and 5 is the y-coordinate of the point A.

- Identify and extend number patterns.

  1, 6, 11, 16, ...

- Identify number relationships between two sets of numbers.

Counting numbers	1	2	3	4	5
Even numbers	2	4	6	8	10

- Graph and compare two sets of data or two patterns on the same coordinate grid.

Name: _____ Date: _____

Solve.

Hunter's Sports sells golf tees from a barrel by the scoop. The golf tees come in 5 bright colors mixed in the barrel. To determine what to charge for each scoop, Ben weighed 15 scoops. The weight of each scoop is shown in the table below.

Weight of Scoop (oz)	1	$1\frac{1}{8}$	$1\frac{1}{4}$	$1\frac{3}{8}$	$1\frac{1}{2}$
Number of Scoops	3	4	5	2	1

1 Use the data to make line plot.

2 What is the total weight of the 15 scoops?

3 If each scoop had exactly the same weight, what would this weight be?

4 If each scoop, containing the 5 colors, had the same weight, between which two weights on the line plot does this weight fall? To which weight is it closer? How do you know?

5 Hunter wants to sell each ounce of tees for $0.50. How much should he charge for each scoop?

Solve.

Dylan uses copper wire to fashion rings for his friends. The data shows the amount of wire he uses to make 10 rings.

Each ✗ represent 1 ring.

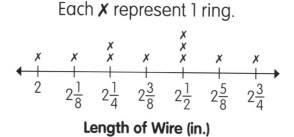

Length of Wire (in.)

6 What is the difference in length between the longest and shortest pieces of wire?

7 Dylan made the 5 shortest rings in one day. How much wire did he use that day?

8 Dylan bought 30 inches of wire. How much wire did he have left after making all the rings?

Use the coordinate plane to answer 9 **to** 13.

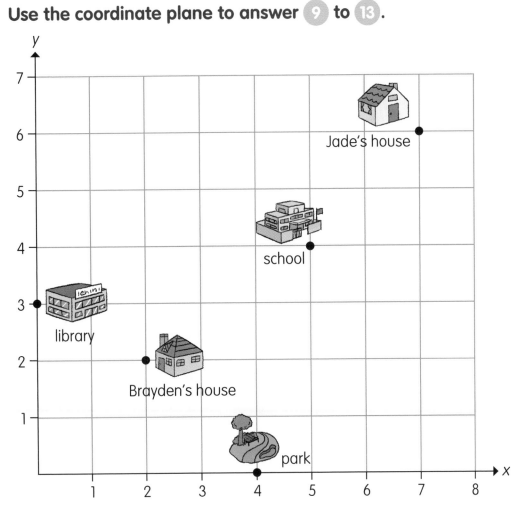

Find the ordered pair that describes each location.

	Location	Ordered Pair
9	Brayden's house	
10	Jade's house	
11	Library	
12	Park	

13 The post office is located at (3, 6). Plot its location on the grid.

14 Plot the points (0, 0), (1, 5), (2, 10), (3, 15), and (4, 20) on the coordinate plane. Use intervals of 2 on the vertical scale.
Join the points. Do you get a straight line graph?
Explain why or why not.

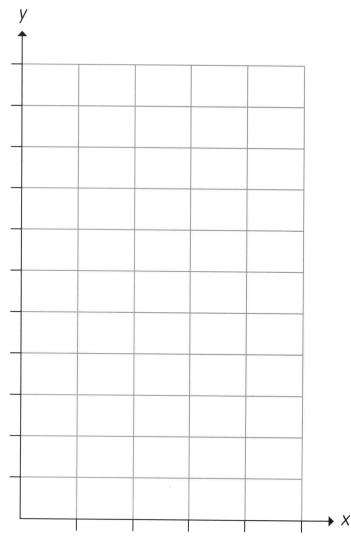

Complete each table. Then, graph the two sets of data, and answer 15 to 19.

Sarah drinks 15 milliliters of milk every second, while Megan drinks 10 milliliters of milk every second. Complete each table below to show the total amount of milk each of them drinks in 5 seconds.

Time (s)	0	1	2	3	4	5
Total Volume of Milk Sarah Drank (mL)	0					

Time (s)	0	1	2	3	4	5
Total Volume of Milk Megan Drank (mL)	0	10				

15 Plot the points of each graph on a coordinate grid. Use increments of 10 on the vertical scale.

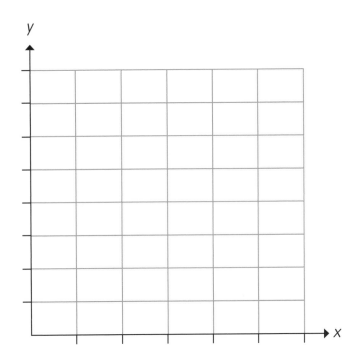

16 How much milk does each person drink in 3 seconds?

17 How long does each person take to drink 60 milliliters of milk?

18 How much milk does each person drink in 7 seconds?

19 Sarah drinks _____ times more than Megan each second.

Use the graph to answer 20 **to** 21 **.**

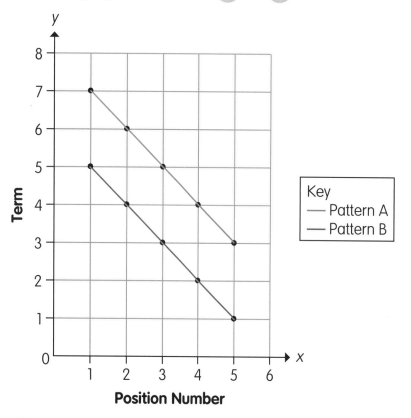

20 Does the point (6, 2) belong to Pattern A or Pattern B?

21 For each value of x from 0 to 6, what can you say about the difference between the y-values for the two patterns?

Assessment Prep

Answer each question.

22 Which statement about the corresponding terms in both Pattern X and Pattern Y is true?

Pattern X: 4, 8, 12, 16, 20, 24 …
Pattern Y: 12, 24, 36, 48, 60, 72 …

(A) Each term in Pattern X is 3 times the corresponding term in Pattern Y.

(B) Each term in Pattern Y is 3 times the corresponding term in Pattern X.

(C) Each term in Pattern X is $\frac{1}{2}$ times the corresponding term in Pattern Y.

(D) Each term in Pattern Y is 8 more than the corresponding term in Pattern X.

23 Which statements correctly describe the coordinate system?
Choose all the correct statements.

(A) The x- and y-axis are perpendicular to each other.

(B) The x- and y-axis are parallel to each other.

(C) The x- and y-axis do not intersect to each other.

(D) The x- and y-axis intersect to each other at the origin.

(E) The ordered pairs are written with the y-coordinate first, followed by the x-coordinate.

(F) The ordered pairs are written with the x-coordinate first, followed by the y-coordinate.

(G) A coordinate plane can be used to locate places on a map.

24 The graph shows the weight of bags of flour.

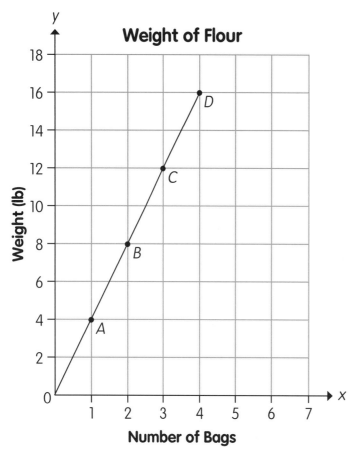

- What are the coordinates of the points *A*, *B*, *C*, and *D*?
- Do either of the points (2, 6) or (4, 14) lie on the graph?
- What is the weight of 10 bags of flour?

Show your answers and explanation in the space below.

Name: _____ Date: _____

Plant Growth

The fifth graders at Best Elementary School are studying the growth of different bean plants.

 The table shows the heights of 17 different bean plants over the course of one week.

Height (in.)	$1\frac{1}{4}$	$1\frac{1}{2}$	$1\frac{3}{4}$	2	$2\frac{1}{4}$
Number of plants	3	5	5	3	1

a   Make a line plot to show the heights of the bean plants.

b   What is the total height of the bean plants? Show your work.

2 Adam records the number of fifth graders and the number of boys in each class in a table as shown.

Class	5A	5B	5C	5D	5E
Number of fifth graders	20	18	22	19	21
Boys	14	12	12	13	13

a Plot the number of girls in each class on the coordinate plane below.

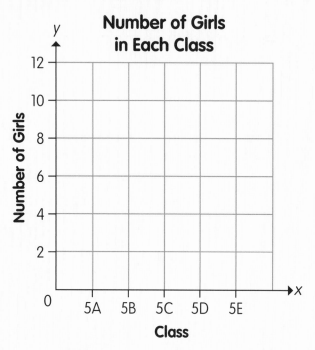

b Describe the number of girls from the five fifth grade classes based on the graph.

3 The bean plants were planted in square plots of different sizes. The table shows the perimeters of the square plots of sides 2 inches, 4 inches, 6 inches, 8 inches, and 10 inches.

Length of Side (inches)	2	4	6	8	10
Perimeter (inches)	8	16	24	32	40

a Plot the points (2, 8), (4, 16), (6, 24), (8, 32), and (10, 40) on the coordinate plane.

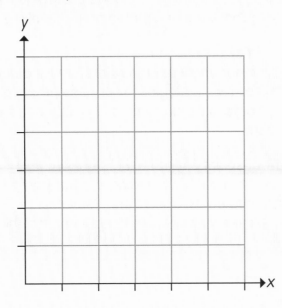

b What do you notice about the points you have plotted?

Rubric

Point(s)	Level	My Performance
7–8	4	• Most of my answers are correct. • I showed complete understanding of what I have learned. • I used the correct strategies to solve the problems. • I explained my answers and mathematical thinking clearly and completely.
5–6	3	• Some of my answers are correct. • I showed some understanding of what I have learned. • I used some correct strategies to solve the problems. • I explained my answers and mathematical thinking clearly.
3–4	2	• A few of my answers are correct. • I showed little understanding of what I have learned. • I used a few correct strategies to solve the problems. • I explained some of my answers and mathematical thinking clearly.
0–2	1	• A few of my answers are correct. • I showed little or no understanding of what I have learned. • I used a few strategies to solve the problems. • I did not explain my answers and mathematical thinking clearly.

Teacher's Comments

How can we classify these objects?

? **What properties can we use to identify triangles? How can we classify polygons using a hierarchy?**

Classifying triangles

Name of Triangle	Definition
Right triangle	Triangle *PQR* is a right triangle. A right triangle has one right angle.
Acute triangle	Triangle *XYZ* is an acute triangle. All the angles in an acute triangle are acute.
Obtuse triangle	Triangle *STU* is an obtuse triangle. An obtuse triangle has an angle that is obtuse.

▶ **Quick Check**

Classify each triangle as right, obtuse, or acute.

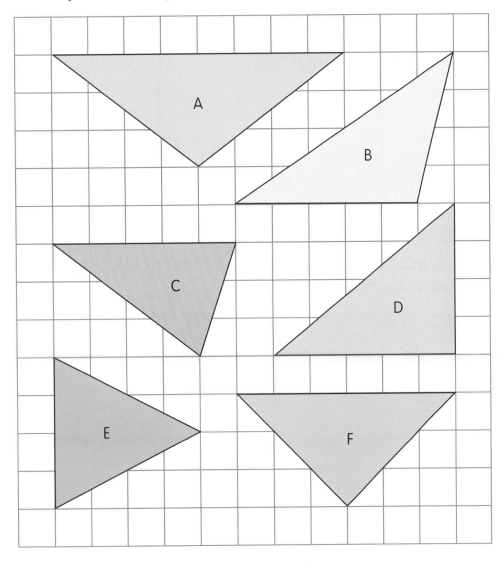

1

Name of Triangle	Triangles
Right triangle	
Acute triangle	
Obtuse triangle	

Classifying polygons

Polygons can be classified in different ways. They can be classified by the presence of parallel sides, size of their angles, or type of polygon they are.

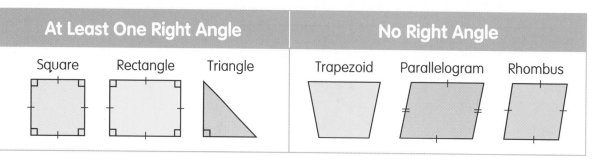

At Least One Right Angle			No Right Angle		
Square	Rectangle	Triangle	Trapezoid	Parallelogram	Rhombus

▶ Quick Check

Sort the polygons into two groups. Write the letter of each polygon in the correct group.

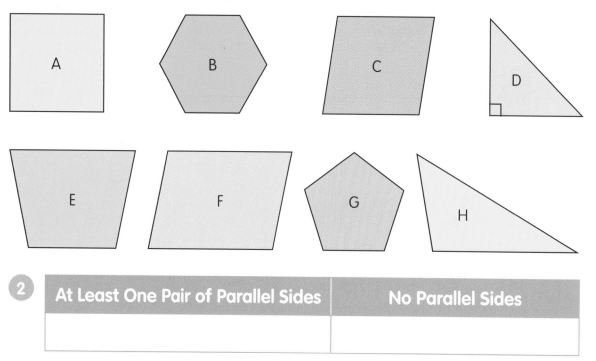

2

At Least One Pair of Parallel Sides	No Parallel Sides

3

Quadrilateral	Not a Quadrilateral

Name: _____   Date: _____

1 Classifying Triangles

Learning Objectives:
- Identify isosceles, equilateral, and scalene triangles.
- Classify triangles by their side lengths and angle measures.

New Vocabulary
equilateral triangle
isosceles triangle
scalene triangle

THINK

a Draw a straight line joining two vertices of the hexagon to make a triangle. Describe the triangle you have made.

b Draw a straight line to join two vertices of the hexagon. Then, draw another straight line to join two other vertices. Describe the triangles you have made.

Repeat **b** with different pairs of straight lines. How many types of triangle can you make? Describe each triangle you have made.

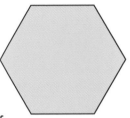

ENGAGE

Draw a triangle with
a 2 equal sides.
b 3 equal sides.
c no equal sides.

What do you notice about the angles in each triangle?

LEARN Identify and classify triangles

1 In triangle *ABC*, all the sides are of equal length.
Triangle *ABC* is an **equilateral triangle**.
In an equilateral triangle, all three angles are equal.

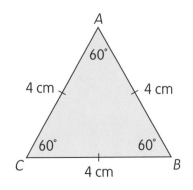

In triangle *ABC*, *AB* = *BC* = *AC*.
Mark the equal sides of the equilateral triangle like this:

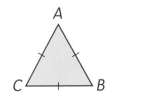

2 In triangle *DEF*, two sides are of equal length.
Triangle *DEF* is an isosceles triangle.
In an isosceles triangle, the angles opposite the equal sides are equal.

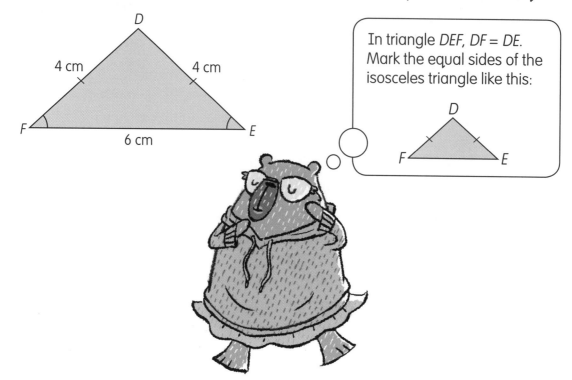

> In triangle *DEF*, *DF* = *DE*.
> Mark the equal sides of the isosceles triangle like this:

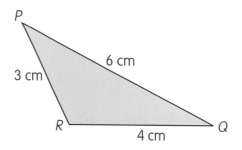

3 In triangle PQR, the three sides have different lengths.
Triangle PQR is a scalene triangle.

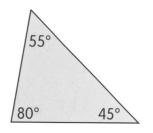

In a scalene triangle, the sizes of all three angles are different.

Look at each triangle.

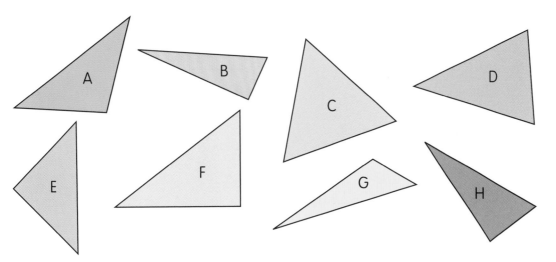

① Measure the side lengths and sizes of each angle in each triangle. Then, fill in the table.

	Acute Triangle	Obtuse Triangle	Right Triangle
Equilateral Triangle			
Isosceles Triangle			
Scalene Triangle			

② **Mathematical Habit 6** Use precise mathematical language

How are the triangles sorted in ① ?

TRY Practice identifying and classifying triangles

Identify each triangle as either *isosceles* **or** *equilateral*.

1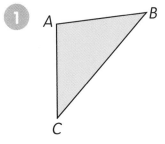

AB = _____ cm

BC = _____ cm

AC = _____ cm

Triangle *ABC* is an _____ triangle.

2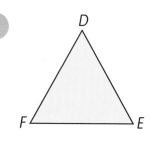

DE = _____ cm

EF = _____ cm

DF = _____ cm

Triangle *DEF* is an _____ triangle.

3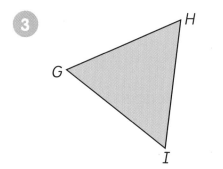

m∠*GHI* = _____ °

m∠*GIH* = _____ °

m∠*HGI* = _____ °

Triangle *GHI* is an _____ triangle.

4

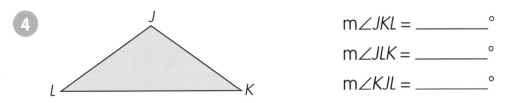

m∠JKL = _____°

m∠JLK = _____°

m∠KJL = _____°

Triangle JKL is an _____ triangle.

Classify each triangle as equilateral, isosceles, or scalene. Choose one name that best describes each triangle.

5

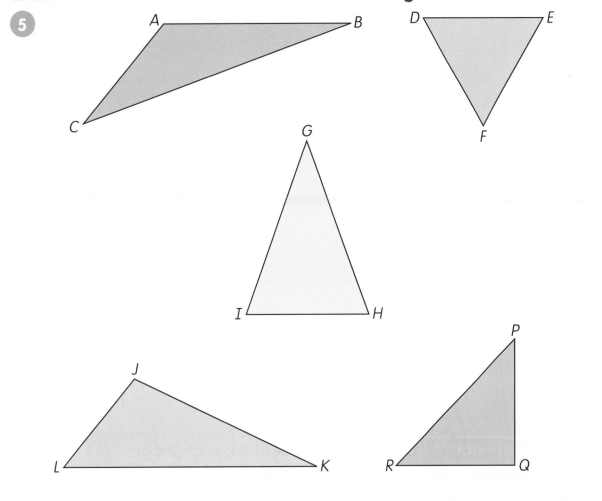

Equilateral Triangle	Isosceles Triangle	Scalene Triangle

Solve.

6 Which triangle does not belong? Explain.

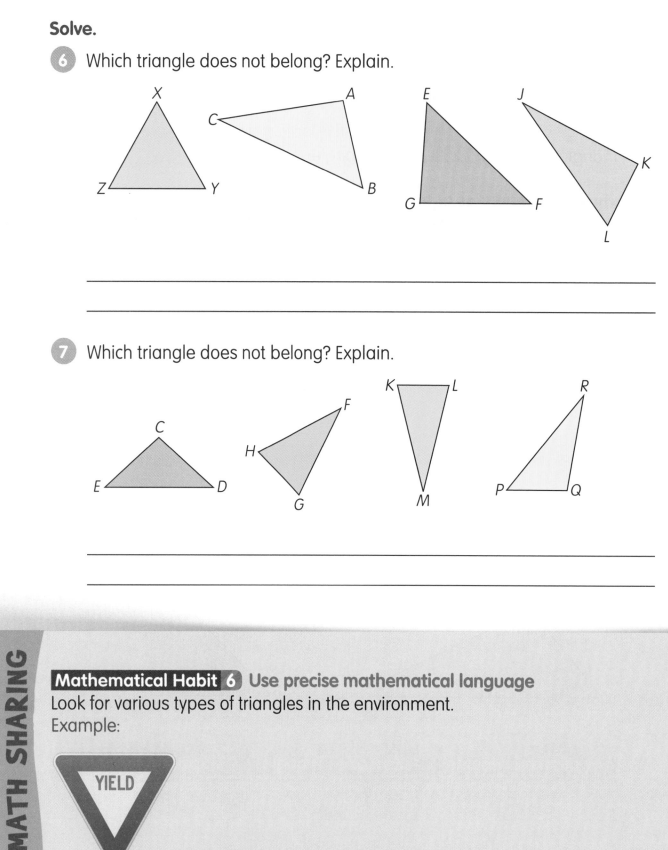

_____

_____

7 Which triangle does not belong? Explain.

_____

_____

Mathematical Habit 6 Use precise mathematical language

Look for various types of triangles in the environment.

Example:

Share and discuss your findings with your partner.

© 2020 Marshall Cavendish Education Pte Ltd

Name: _____ Date: _____

INDEPENDENT PRACTICE

Identify each triangle as either isosceles or equilateral.

1

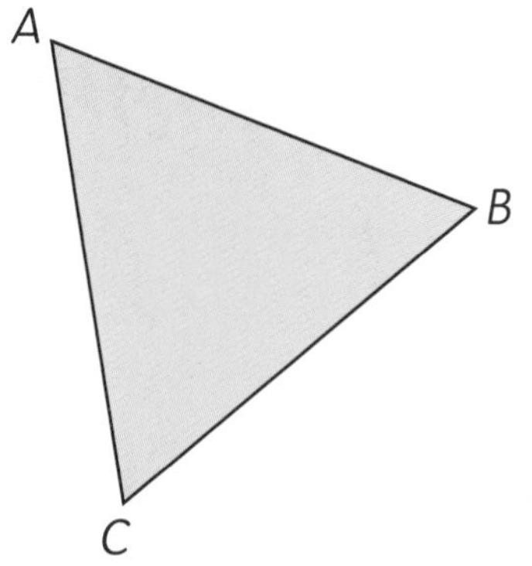

A

B

C

AB = _____ cm

BC = _____ cm

AC = _____ cm

Triangle *ABC* is an _____ triangle.

2

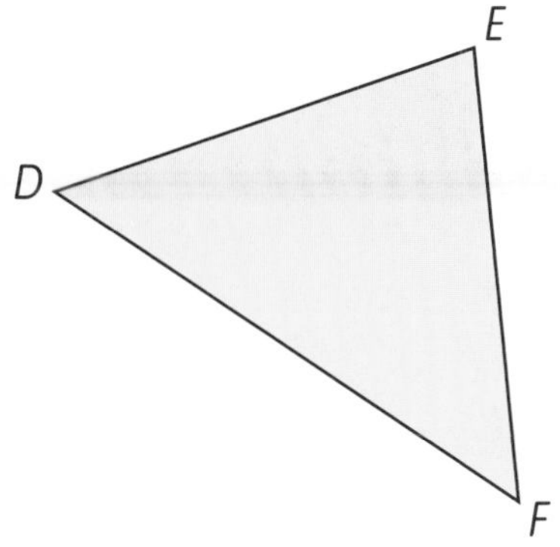

E

D

F

DE = _____ cm

EF = _____ cm

DF = _____ cm

Triangle *DEF* is an _____ triangle.

3

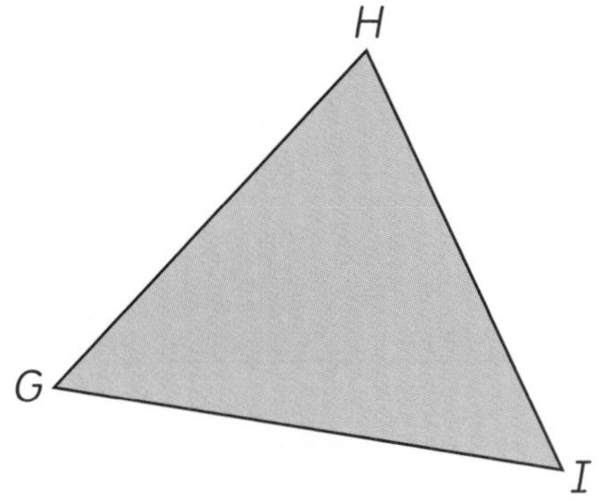

H

G

I

m∠*GHI* = _____ °

m∠*GIH* = _____ °

m∠*HGI* = _____ °

Triangle *GHI* is an _____ triangle.

Classify each triangle as equilateral, isosceles, or scalene.
Choose one name that best describes each triangle.

4

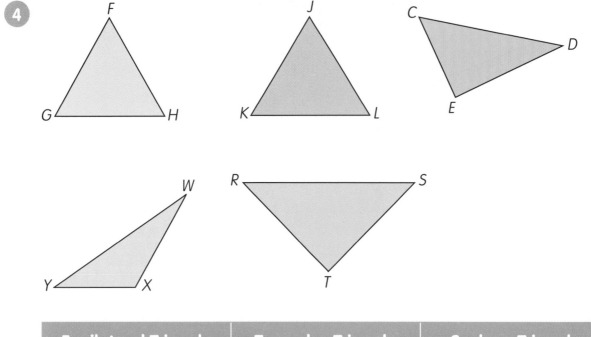

Equilateral Triangle	Isosceles Triangle	Scalene Triangle

Solve.

5 Which triangle does not belong? Explain.

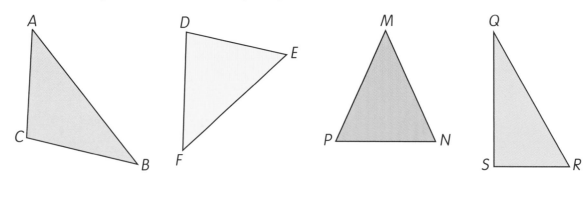

_____

_____

2 Classifying Polygons

Learning Objective:
• Classify polygons using a hierarchy.

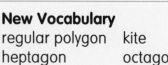

New Vocabulary

regular polygon   kite
heptagon   octagon
nonagon   decagon

THINK

All squares are rhombuses. All squares are rectangles.
So, are all rhombuses rectangles? Explain.

ENGAGE

Draw 2 different shapes with four equal sides. How are they the same?
How are they different?

LEARN Classify polygons and their hierarchy

1. When all sides of a polygon are equal and all the angles within the
   polygon are equal, the polygon is called a regular polygon.

Regular Polygon	Not a Regular Polygon
All sides are congruent or equal.	Not all sides are congruent or equal.
All angles are congruent or equal.	Not all angles are congruent or equal.
Examples:	Examples:

2 Polygons can be put into a hierarchy as shown.

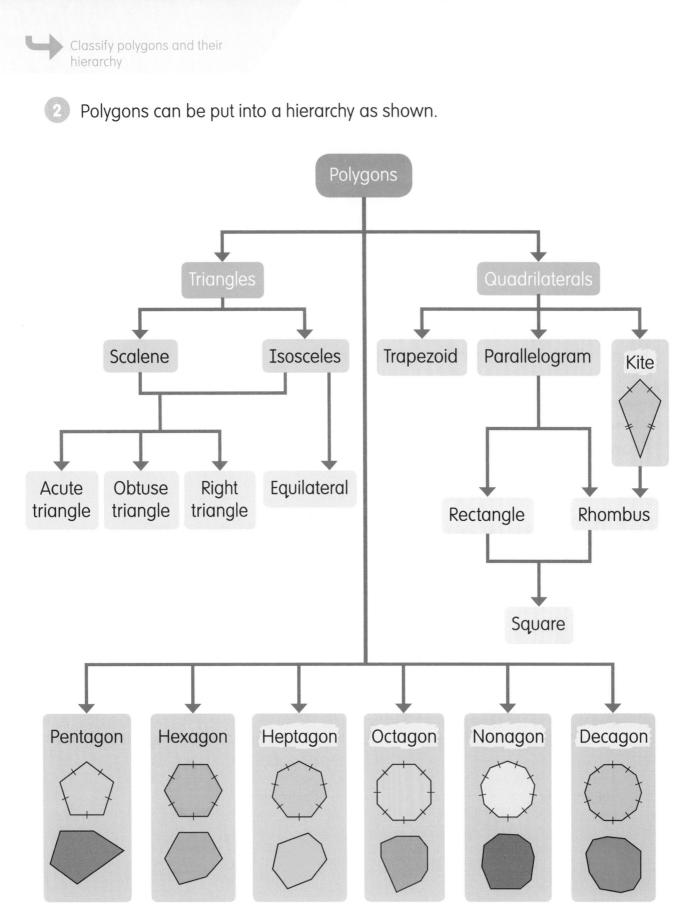

TRY Practice classifying polygons and their hierarchy

Name each polygon. Identify whether each is a regular polygon.

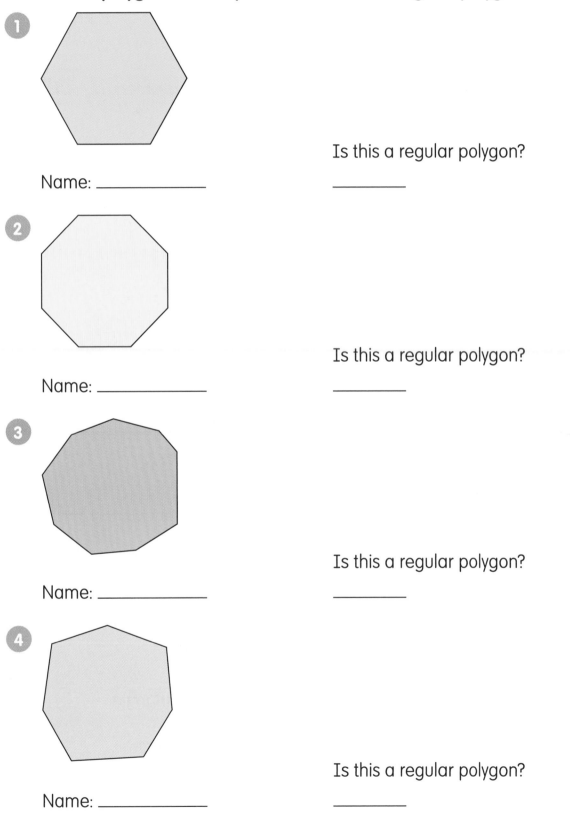

1

Name: _____

Is this a regular polygon?

_____

2

Name: _____

Is this a regular polygon?

_____

3

Name: _____

Is this a regular polygon?

_____

4

Is this a regular polygon?

_____

Name: _____

Classify each polygon in as many ways as possible. Write quadrilateral,
trapezoid, parallelogram, rectangle, rhombus, kite, **or** square.

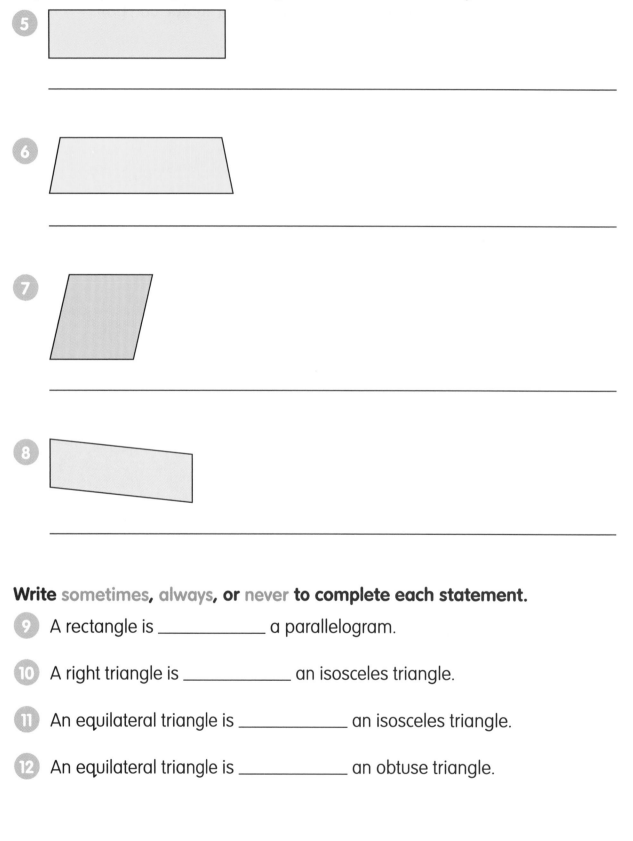

⑤

_____

⑥

_____

⑦

_____

⑧

_____

Write sometimes, always, **or** never **to complete each statement.**

⑨ A rectangle is _____ a parallelogram.

⑩ A right triangle is _____ an isosceles triangle.

⑪ An equilateral triangle is _____ an isosceles triangle.

⑫ An equilateral triangle is _____ an obtuse triangle.

INDEPENDENT PRACTICE

Name each polygon. Identify whether each is a regular polygon.

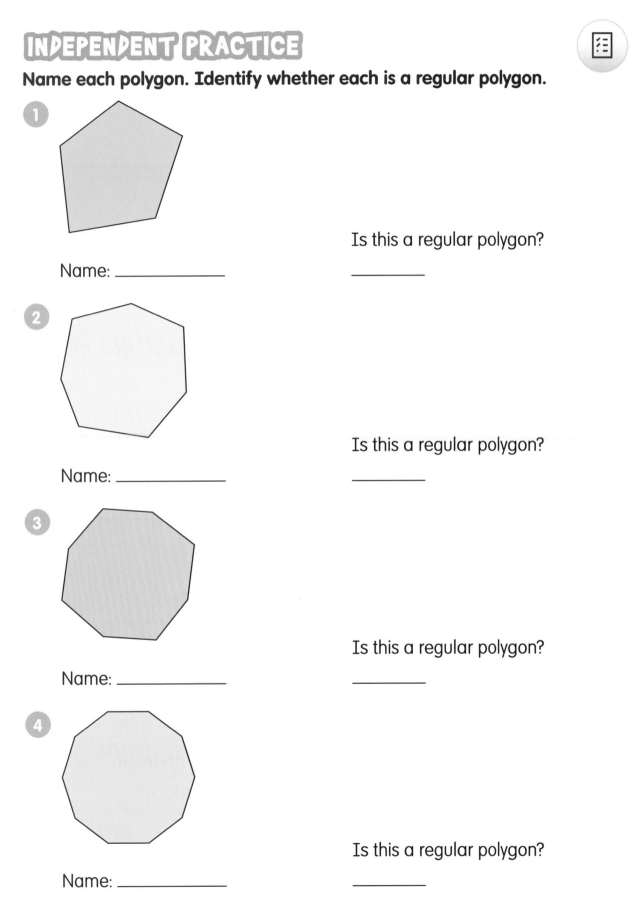

1

Name: _____

Is this a regular polygon?

_____

2

Name: _____

Is this a regular polygon?

_____

3

Name: _____

Is this a regular polygon?

_____

4

Name: _____

Is this a regular polygon?

_____

Classify each polygon in as many ways as possible. Write quadrilateral, trapezoid, parallelogram, rectangle, rhombus, kite, **or** square.

5 _____

6 _____

Classify each triangle in as many ways as possible. Write scalene, isosceles, equilateral, right, acute, **or** obtuse.

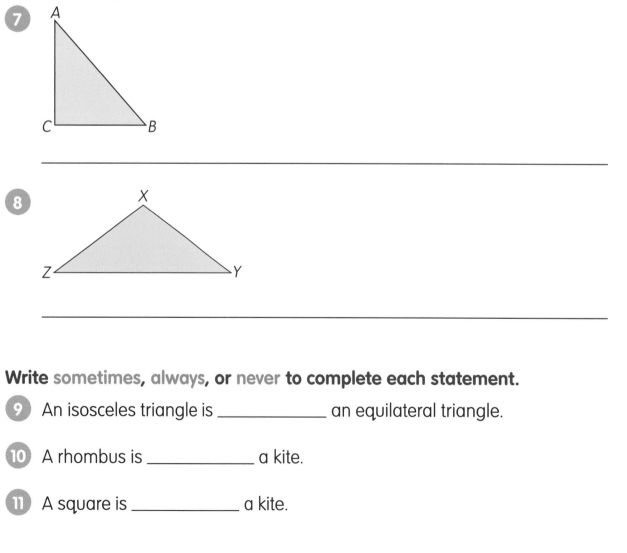

7 _____

8 _____

Write sometimes, always, **or** never **to complete each statement.**

9 An isosceles triangle is _____ an equilateral triangle.

10 A rhombus is _____ a kite.

11 A square is _____ a kite.

Mathematical Habit 3 Construct viable arguments

Julian wrote the following sentences.

1. A right triangle can be a scalene or an isosceles triangle.

2. An equilateral triangle can sometimes be a scalene triangle.

3. A rhombus is not a parallelogram.

4. A rectangle is always a parallelogram.

5. A parallelogram is also a trapezoid.

Explain if the sentences are true or false.

Problem Solving with Heuristics

1 **Mathematical Habit 6** Use precise mathematical language

How many different kinds of quadrilateral can be made by joining the dots on the circle?

2 **Mathematical Habit** 6 Use precise mathematical language

List the polygons that you can identify in the picture.

CHAPTER WRAP-UP

?

What properties can we use to identify triangles? How can we classify polygons using a hierarchy?

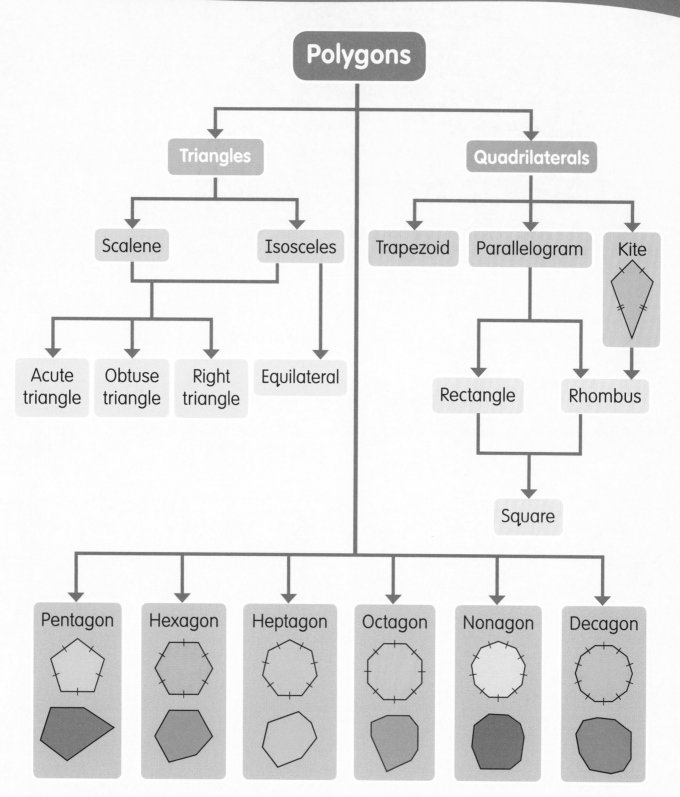

Name: _____   Date: _____

Classify each triangle. Choose one name that best describes each triangle.

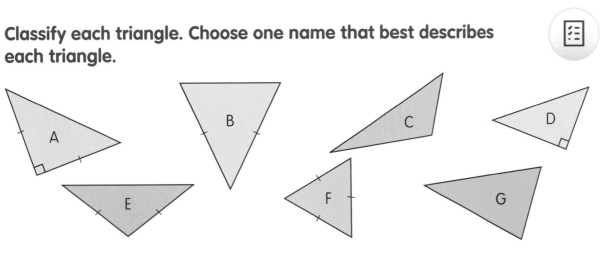

1

Equilateral Triangle	Isosceles Triangle	Scalene Triangle

2

Acute Triangle	Obtuse Triangle	Right Triangle

Name the polygon. Identify whether it is a regular polygon.

3

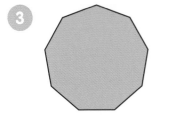

Is this a regular polygon?

Name: _____   _____

Classify each polygon in as many ways as possible. Write quadrilateral, trapezoid, parallelogram, rectangle, rhombus, kite, **or** square.

4

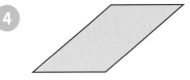

_____
_____

5

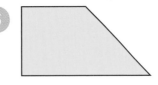

_____
_____

Classify each triangle in as many ways as possible. Write scalene, isosceles, equilateral, right, acute, **or** obtuse.

6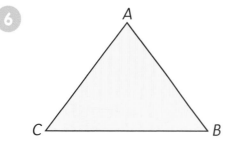

7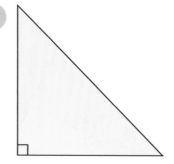

_____

_____

Assessment Prep

Answer each question.

8 Which figure is never a parallelogram?

Ⓐ square

Ⓑ rhombus

Ⓒ rectangle

Ⓓ trapezoid

9 Which statements about figures are correct?

Ⓐ All kites are rhombuses.

Ⓑ All squares are parallelograms.

Ⓒ All parallelograms have two pairs of parallel sides.

Ⓓ All kites have two pairs of equal sides.

Ⓔ All rectangles are squares.

10 A quadrilateral has only two equal sides. What kind of quadrilateral can it be? Explain.

Name: _____ Date: _____

Classifying Polygons

1 Fill in each blank with the name that best describes each polygon. Use each name from the list only once.

rectangle	right triangle	square
scalene triangle	rhombus	isosceles triangle
parallelogram	equilateral triangle	trapezoid

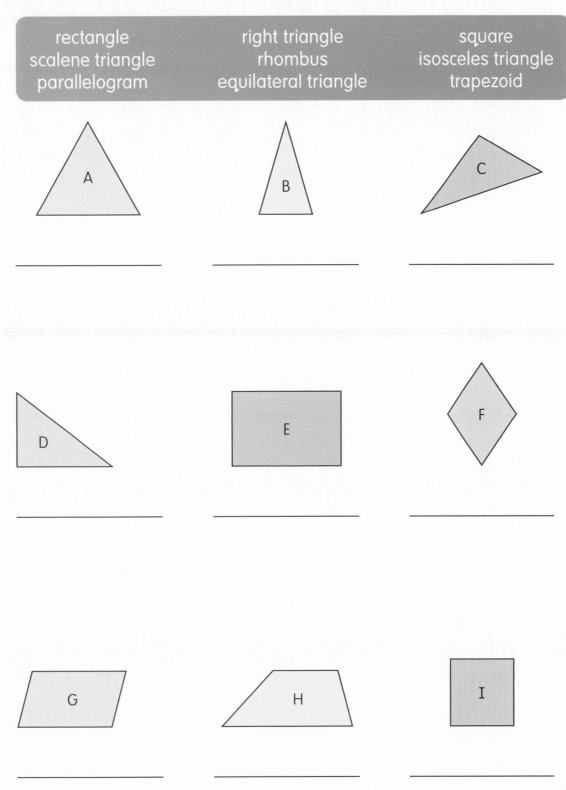

A _____ B _____ C _____

D _____ E _____ F _____

G _____ H _____ I _____

2 Use the figures in ① to fill in the table.

Figures with all sides equal	Figures with all angles equal	Figures with opposite sides equal	Figures with no equal sides	Figures with at least one right angle	Figures with at least one pair of parallel sides	Figures with at least two equal sides

Rubric

Point(s)	Level	My Performance
7–8	4	• Most of my answers are correct. • I showed complete understanding of what I have learned. • I used the correct strategies to solve the problems. • I explained my answers and mathematical thinking clearly and completely.
5–6	3	• Some of my answers are correct. • I showed some understanding of what I have learned. • I used some correct strategies to solve the problems. • I explained my answers and mathematical thinking clearly.
3–4	2	• A few of my answers are correct. • I showed little understanding of what I have learned. • I used a few correct strategies to solve the problems. • I explained some of my answers and mathematical thinking clearly.
0–2	1	• A few of my answers are correct. • I showed little or no understanding of what I have learned. • I used a few strategies to solve the problems. • I did not explain my answers and mathematical thinking clearly.

Teacher's Comments

STEAM

Cubism

Cubism was an art movement that began in the early 1900s in Paris. Artists Pablo Picasso and Georges Braque were leaders in the movement. They created a new way to look at the world. They used angular geometric shapes to paint objects and landscapes. Form was more important than color.

Task

Create an Image in the Cubist Style

Work in pairs or independently to learn about cubism and to create an original piece of cubist work.

1. Go online or to the library to learn more about cubism. Find examples of cubist art.

2. Take a photograph of an interesting object or landscape. Use traditional art materials or digital tools to create a piece of art in the cubist style.

3. If you choose to use traditional art materials, print your photograph on the largest piece of paper possible. Use a ruler, pencil, and scissors to divide your image into polygonal shapes. Use different kinds of polygons. Rearrange and glue your shapes onto a piece of art paper. Create interesting spaces between the shapes.

4. If you choose to use digital tools, go online to the Columbus Museum of Art. Use the museum's web app that turns photos into cubist works of art. Follow the easy steps. Save and print your image.

5. Add your work to a cubist art wall in your classroom.

Ratio

How can you relate and compare two or three quantities?

Name: _____ Date: _____

Comparing numbers using subtraction

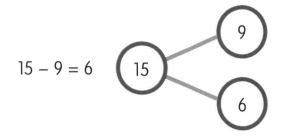

15 − 9 = 6

6 is 9 less than 15.

15 is 9 more than 6.

▶ Quick Check

Use the number bond to fill in each blank.

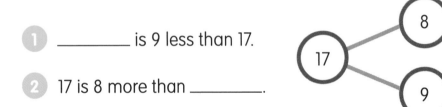

1. _____ is 9 less than 17.

2. 17 is 8 more than _____.

Understanding fractions

A fraction is part of a whole.

The numerator represents the number of parts and the denominator represents the whole.

$\frac{3}{5}$ is 3 out of 5 parts.

▶ Quick Check

State how many parts of the whole are represented by each fraction.

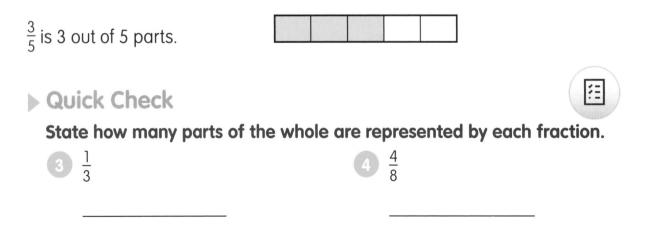

3. $\frac{1}{3}$

    _____

4. $\frac{4}{8}$

    _____

Writing fractions in simplest form

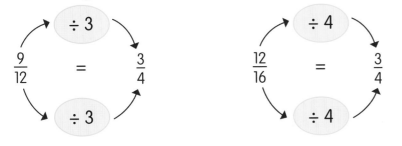

Divide the numerator and denominator by their common factor.

▶ **Quick Check**

Write each fraction in simplest form.

5 $\dfrac{15}{20}$

6 $\dfrac{18}{21}$

7 $\dfrac{4}{24}$

8 $\dfrac{27}{36}$

Using a bar model to solve problems

Find the value of each set using the bar model.

a   4 units
b   1 unit
c   3 units
d   7 units

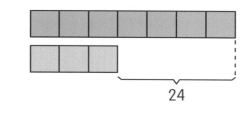

From the model:

a   4 units = 24

b   1 unit = 24 ÷ 4
            = 6

c   3 units = 6 × 3
            = 18

d   7 units = 6 × 7
            = 42

▶ Quick Check

Use the bar model to find the value of each set.

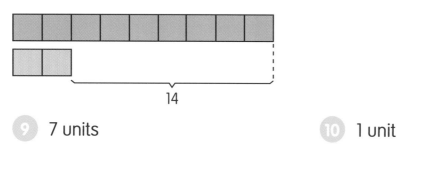

14

9 7 units

10 1 unit

11 2 units

12 9 units

1 Finding Ratio

Learning Objective:
• Read and write ratios.

> **New Vocabulary**
> ratio

THINK

Charlotte cuts a ribbon into two pieces. The first piece is twice as long as the second piece. Draw a model to represent the two pieces of ribbon. How can you write the lengths as a ratio of each other? What is a possible length of the original piece of ribbon?

ENGAGE

a Take some ⚪⚪. Separate them into two groups of different colors. Write a statement to relate the number of counters in the two groups.

b Create another two groups for your partner. Ask your partner to write a statement to relate the number of counters in the two new groups.

LEARN Use ratios to compare two quantities

1 There are 2 pens and 3 pencils.

The ratio of the number of pens to the number of pencils is 2 : 3.
2 : 3 is read as 2 to 3.

The ratio of the number of pencils to the number of pens is 3 : 2.
3 : 2 is read as 3 to 2.

Hands-on Activity Writing ratio statements to compare two quantities

Work in pairs.

(1) Take a handful of ⬤ and ◯.

(2) Ask your partner to count the number of red counters and yellow counters. Then, write two ratio statements to describe the counters.

(3) Trade places. Repeat (1) and (2).

TRY Practice using ratios to compare two quantities

Fill in each blank.

1

The ratio of the number of yellow beads to the number of green beads

is _____ : _____.

The ratio of the number of green beads to the number of yellow beads

is _____ : _____.

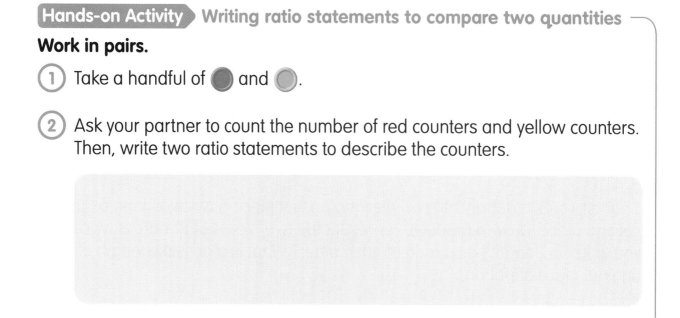

2

The ratio of the number of blue pennants to the number of

yellow pennants is _____ : _____.

The ratio of the number of yellow pennants to the number of

blue pennants is _____ : _____.

ENGAGE

Take 3 groups of 2 🔵 and 5 groups of 2 ⚪. How can you write the ratio of number of blue counters to the number of yellow counters in different ways? Explain your ideas to your partner.

LEARN Use ratios to compare two sets of objects

1 Makayla bought 3 packs of carrots and 4 packs of cucumbers.

1 unit   1 unit

The number of items in each pack is the same.
Each pack represents one unit.
A ratio may not give the actual number of carrots and cucumbers.

The ratio of the number of carrots to the number of cucumbers is 3 : 4.

The ratio of the number of cucumbers to the number of carrots is 4 : 3.

Math Talk

Ava and Joshua were each given 6 trays, 5 blue counters, and 25 green counters to show the ratio 1 : 5.
Ava placed 1 blue counter on 1 tray and 1 green counter on each of the 5 trays.
Joshua placed 5 blue counters on 1 tray and 5 green counters on each of the 5 trays.

How are the two ways shown by Ava and Joshua different? Discuss with your partner.

TRY Practice using ratios to compare two sets of objects

Fill in each blank.

1

1 unit represents _____ packets of juice.

1 unit represents the number of packets of grape juice.

_____ units represent the number of packets of apple juice.

The ratio of the number of packets of grape juice to the number of packets

of apple juice is _____ : _____.

The ratio of the number of packets of apple juice to the number of packets

of grape juice is _____ : _____.

2

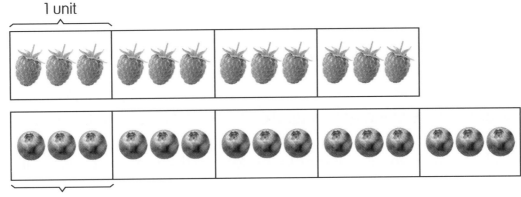

1 unit

1 unit

The ratio of the number of raspberries to the number of blueberries

is _____ : _____.

The ratio of the number of blueberries to the number of raspberries

is _____ : _____.

ENGAGE

William has 3 kilograms of rice and Addison has 720 grams of rice. Kylie says
720 grams is heavier than 3 kilograms because 720 is greater than 3.
Is she correct? Explain.

LEARN Use ratios to compare two measurements in the same unit

1 Bryan buys 2 kilograms of chicken and 9 kilograms of ham.

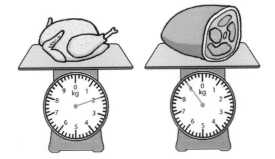

To compare the masses,
they must be in the same
unit. However, we do not
include the unit in the ratio.

The ratio of the mass of chicken to the mass of ham is 2 : 9.

The ratio of the mass of ham to the mass of chicken is 9 : 2.

TRY Practice using ratios to compare two measurements in the same unit

Fill in each blank.

1 There are 15 liters of water in a tank and 8 liters of water in a pail.

The ratio of the amount of water in the tank to the amount of water in

the pail is _____ : _____.

The ratio of the amount of water in the pail to the amount of water in

the tank is _____ : _____.

ENGAGE

Measure the length of your pencil correct to the nearest centimeter.
Compare the length of your pencil to the length of your partner's pencil.
What ratios could you write to describe the relationship between the lengths?
Write the ratios for each relationship.

LEARN Use ratios to compare units

1

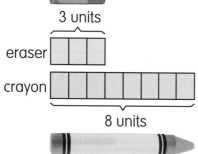

The ratio of the length of the eraser to the length of the crayon is 3 : 8.
The ratio of the length of the crayon to the length of the eraser is 8 : 3.

The ratio of the length of the eraser to the total length of the eraser and the crayon is 3 : 11.

What is the ratio of the length of the crayon to the total length of the eraser and the crayon?

Work in pairs.

(1) Draw a bar model to show the ratio 7 : 3.

(2) Ask your partner to use 🧊 to show the ratio 7 : 3. Your partner writes another three ratios about the cubes shown and describes them.

Example: The ratio of the number of blue cubes to the total number of cubes is 3 : 10.

(3) Trade places. Repeat (1) and (2) with the ratio 4 : 6.

TRY Practice using ratios to compare units

Fill in each blank.

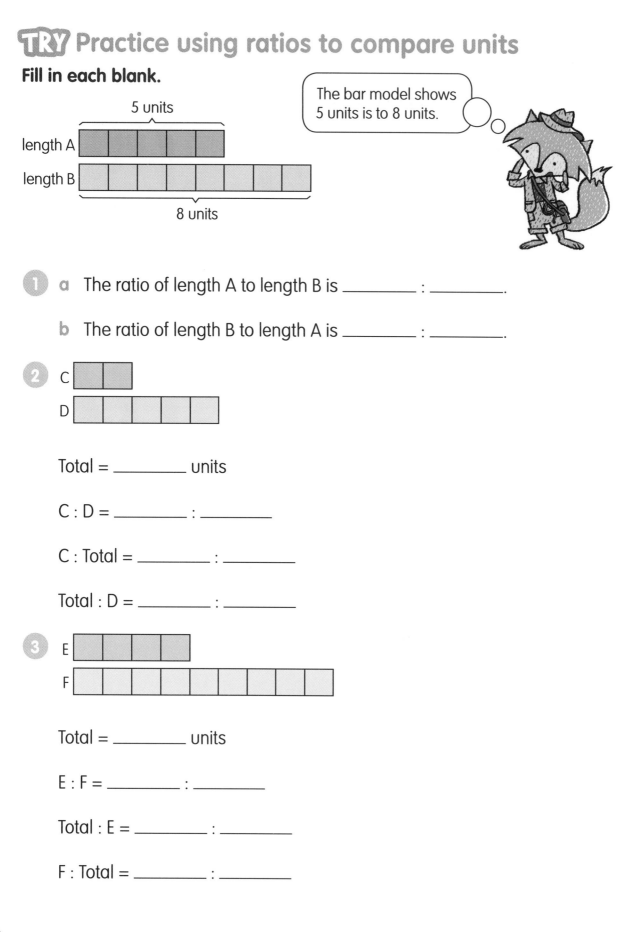

The bar model shows 5 units is to 8 units.

1 **a** The ratio of length A to length B is _____ : _____.

b The ratio of length B to length A is _____ : _____.

2 C

D

Total = _____ units

C : D = _____ : _____

C : Total = _____ : _____

Total : D = _____ : _____

3 E

F

Total = _____ units

E : F = _____ : _____

Total : E = _____ : _____

F : Total = _____ : _____

ENGAGE

Fold a rectangular piece of paper three times to form 8 equal parts. Shade any number of parts but not all of them. How would you draw a model to show the ratio of the number of shaded parts to the number of unshaded parts? What other ratios could you write? Share with your partner.

LEARN Use a part-whole model to show a ratio

1 Ryan cut a piece of wood, 24 centimeters long, into two pieces. The shorter piece was 7 centimeters long. Find the ratio of the length of the shorter piece to the length of the longer piece.

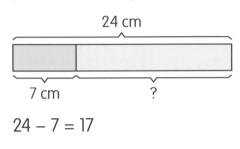

24 cm

7 cm   ?

24 − 7 = 17

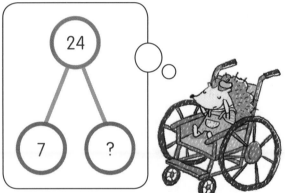

The length of the longer piece of wood was 17 centimeters.

The ratio of the length of the shorter piece to the length of the longer piece was 7 : 17.

Hands-on Activity Drawing part-whole models to represent ratios

Work in pairs.

1 Take 20 and connect them to form a row. Then, disconnect the row into two parts in any way.

2 Ask your partner to write two ratios about the two parts formed from the 20 cubes.

3 Trade places. Repeat 1 and 2 with different number of cubes in each part.

TRY Practice using a part-whole model to show a ratio

Fill in each blank.

1 Mr. Smith had 19 pounds of green beans to sell at his vegetable stall. He sold 11 pounds of green beans. Find the ratio of the weight of green beans sold to the weight of green beans left.

19 – _____ = _____

The mass of green beans left was _____ pounds.

The ratio of the mass of green beans sold to the mass of

green beans left was _____ : _____.

Name: _____ Date: _____

INDEPENDENT PRACTICE

Write each ratio.

1. The ratio of the number of blue balloons to the number of yellow balloons

   is _____ : _____.

2. The ratio of the number of yellow balloons to the number of blue balloons

   is _____ : _____.

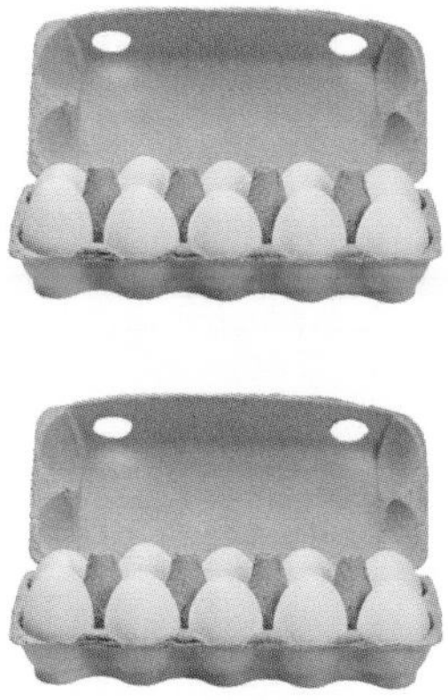

Set A 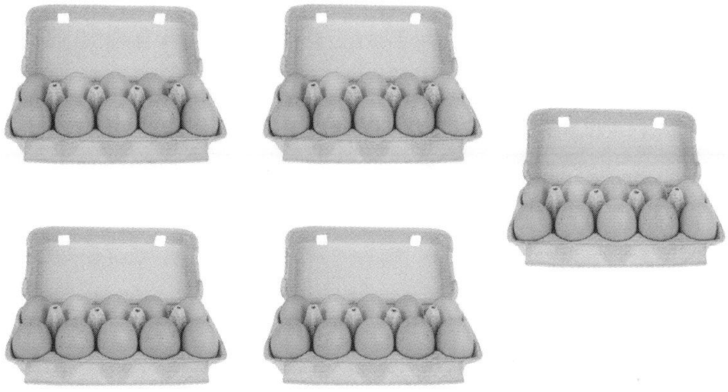   Set B

3. The ratio of the number of brown eggs to the number of white eggs

   is _____ : _____.

4. The ratio of the number of white eggs to the number of brown eggs

   is _____ : _____.

The table shows the masses of shellfish sold at a seafood market one afternoon.

Shellfish	Mussels	Shrimp	Crabs	Lobsters	Scallops
Mass	2 kg	5 kg	3 kg	11 kg	8 kg

Use the data in the table to fill in each blank in 5 and 6.
Then, write another six ratios in the box provided in 7.

	Ratio
Mass of mussels to mass of shrimp	2 : 5
5 Mass of lobsters to mass of scallops	_____ : _____
6 Mass of crabs to mass of shellfish in total	_____ : _____

7 Example: Mass of mussels to mass of lobsters = 2 : 11

Draw a model to show the ratio.

Example:

A : B = 2 : 5   A [ ][ ]
                     B [ ][ ][ ][ ][ ]

8 A : B = 11 : 7

Write two ratios to compare Set A and Set B.

9

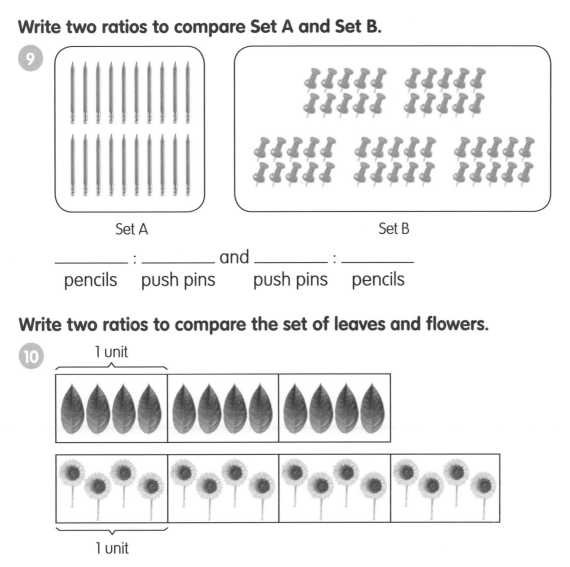

Set A   Set B

_____ : _____ and _____ : _____
pencils   push pins   push pins   pencils

Write two ratios to compare the set of leaves and flowers.

10

1 unit

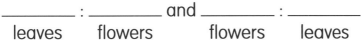

1 unit

_____ : _____ and _____ : _____
leaves   flowers   flowers   leaves

Draw a model to show the ratio. Then, fill in each blank.

11 A : B = 4 : 9

a Model:

b Total = _____ units

c A : Total = _____ : _____

d Total : B = _____ : _____

Solve.

12 A large checkered tablecloth is 5 feet wide and 7 feet long. Find the ratio of the length of the tablecloth to its width.

13 James has $88. He gives $35 to charity A and the rest to charity B. Find the ratio of the amount of money he gives to charity A to the amount of money he gives to charity B.

Name: _____   Date: _____

2 Equivalent Ratios

Learning Objectives:
- Find equivalent ratios using multiplication or division.
- Solve ratio problems using multiplication or division.

> **New Vocabulary**
> equivalent ratios
> simplest form

THINK

The ratio of the number of dimes to the number of nickels is 10 : 5.

a Yong took 2 dimes. How many nickels must be removed to keep the ratio equivalent to 10 : 5?

b If he took 2 coins away from each group, is the new ratio equivalent to 10 : 5?

ENGAGE

You are given 12 ⬤ and 24 ⬤. Is it possible to create the ratio 1 : 2 by using all the counters? What about 3 : 4? How do you know? Use the counters to justify your reasoning.

LEARN Write equivalent ratios

1 Nora has 4 apples and 8 pears.

The ratio of the number of apples to the number of pears is 4 : 8.

Nora puts the fruits onto trays of 2.

The ratio of the number of apples to the number of pears is 2 : 4.

Nora then puts the fruits onto trays of 4.

The ratio of the number of apples to the number of pears is 1 : 2.

4 : 8, 2 : 4, and 1 : 2 are equivalent ratios.

TRY Practice writing equivalent ratios

Fill in each blank.

1

The ratio of the number of blue counters to the number of red counters

is _____ : _____.

2

The ratio of the number of blue counters to the number of red counters

is _____ : _____.

3

The ratio of the number of blue counters to the number of red counters

is _____ : _____.

4 There are 8 coins. Separate them into two sets with an even number of coins in each set. Write 2 equivalent ratios to compare the two sets.

_____ : _____ and _____ : _____

Find all the common factors for each of the following pairs of numbers.

a 4 and 2   b 8 and 12
c 12 and 18   d 44 and 121

LEARN Use multiplication and division to find equivalent ratios

1 You can multiply the quantities in a ratio by the same number to find an equivalent ratio.

$$\times 2 \begin{pmatrix} 1:3 \\ 2:6 \end{pmatrix} \times 2 \qquad \times 3 \begin{pmatrix} 1:3 \\ 3:9 \end{pmatrix} \times 3$$

You can also find equivalent ratios by expressing ratios in their simplest forms.

$$\div 2 \begin{pmatrix} 2:6 \\ = 1:3 \end{pmatrix} \div 2 \qquad \div 3 \begin{pmatrix} 3:9 \\ = 1:3 \end{pmatrix} \div 3$$

> A ratio is in its simplest form when all its terms do not have a common factor other than 1.

1 and 3 do not have a common factor other than 1.

So, 1 : 3 is the simplest form of 2 : 6 and 3 : 9.

TRY Practice using multiplication and division to find equivalent ratios

Fill in each blank to express each ratio in simplest form.

1

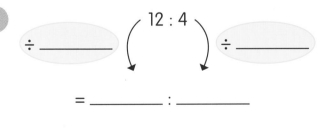

$$\div \underline{\hspace{2cm}} \begin{pmatrix} 12:4 \end{pmatrix} \div \underline{\hspace{2cm}}$$

$$= \underline{\hspace{2cm}} : \underline{\hspace{2cm}}$$

> The common factor of 12 and 4 is _____.
>
> Divide 12 and 4 by _____.

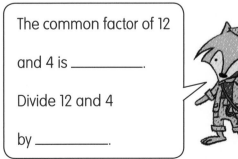

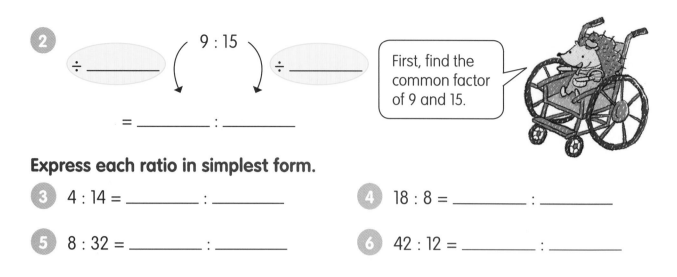

②

$$\div \rule{2cm}{0.4pt} \quad 9 : 15 \quad \div \rule{2cm}{0.4pt}$$

$$= \rule{2cm}{0.4pt} : \rule{2cm}{0.4pt}$$

> First, find the common factor of 9 and 15.

Express each ratio in simplest form.

③ 4 : 14 = _____ : _____

④ 18 : 8 = _____ : _____

⑤ 8 : 32 = _____ : _____

⑥ 42 : 12 = _____ : _____

ENGAGE

What are two possible values of A and B in each of the following? Discuss with your partner.

a   7 : A = B : 21

b   42 : A = B : 28

LEARN Find an unknown value of an equivalent ratio

① Find the missing number.
2 : 5 = 6 : ?

▶ **Method 1**

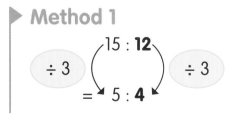

$$\times 3 \quad \begin{pmatrix} \mathbf{2} : 5 \\ = \mathbf{6} : 15 \end{pmatrix} \quad \times 3$$

The missing number is 15.

▶ **Method 2**

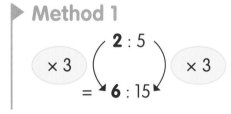

$$\div 3 \quad \begin{pmatrix} \mathbf{2} : 5 \\ = 6 : 15 \end{pmatrix} \quad \div 3$$

② Find the missing number.
15 : 12 = ? : 4

▶ **Method 1**

$$\div 3 \quad \begin{pmatrix} 15 : \mathbf{12} \\ = 5 : \mathbf{4} \end{pmatrix} \quad \div 3$$

The missing number is 5.

▶ **Method 2**

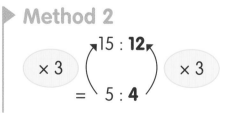

$$\times 3 \quad \begin{pmatrix} 15 : \mathbf{12} \\ = 5 : \mathbf{4} \end{pmatrix} \quad \times 3$$

Work in pairs.

1. Take 14 ⬛ and 28 ⬛. Put the colored cubes into groups so that each group has the same number of cubes. (Do not mix yellow cubes and red cubes in a group.)

2. Ask your partner to write the ratio of the number of groups of ⬛ to the number of groups of ⬛.

3. Repeat ① and ② with different number of cubes in each group to get another two ratios.

4. **Mathematical Habit 8** **Look for patterns**

   What can you say about the ratios in ② and ③?

5. Trade places. Repeat the activity using 8 ⬛ and 24 ⬛.

6. What can you say about these ratios? Why is this so? Explain your reasoning.

TRY Practice finding an unknown value of an equivalent ratio

Find the missing terms in each set of equivalent ratios.

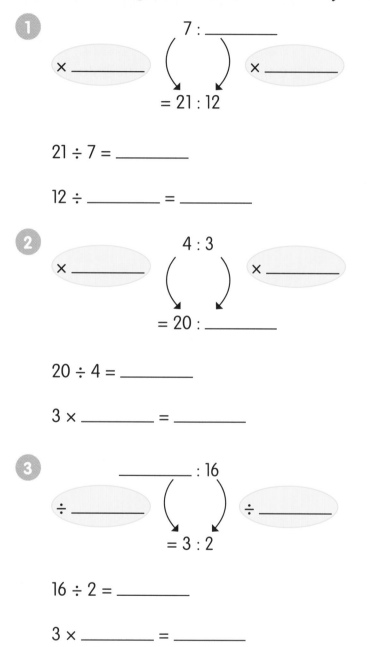

1

× _____   7 : _____   × _____

= 21 : 12

21 ÷ 7 = _____

12 ÷ _____ = _____

2

× _____   4 : 3   × _____

= 20 : _____

20 ÷ 4 = _____

3 × _____ = _____

3

÷ _____   _____ : 16   ÷ _____

= 3 : 2

16 ÷ 2 = _____

3 × _____ = _____

Fill in each blank.

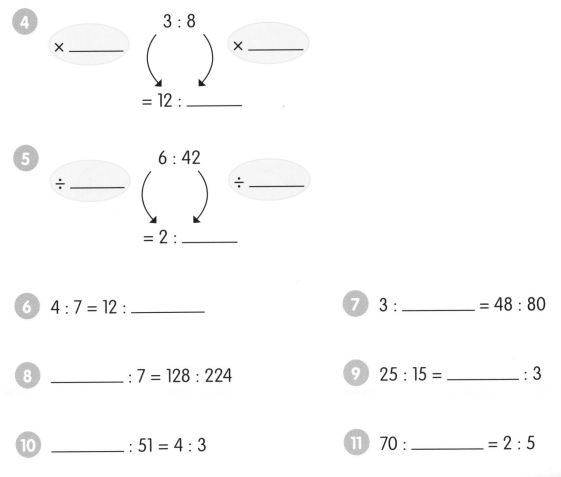

4

$\times$ _____ $3 : 8$ $\times$ _____

$= 12 :$ _____

5

$\div$ _____ $6 : 42$ $\div$ _____

$= 2 :$ _____

6 $4 : 7 = 12 :$ _____

7 $3 :$ _____ $= 48 : 80$

8 _____ $: 7 = 128 : 224$

9 $25 : 15 =$ _____ $: 3$

10 _____ $: 51 = 4 : 3$

11 $70 :$ _____ $= 2 : 5$

Mathematical Habit **8** Use precise mathematical language

Express $\frac{4}{10}$ and $4 : 10$ in their simplest forms.

Discuss with your partner the similarity between expressing fractions and expressing ratios in their simplest forms.

© 2020 Marshall Cavendish Education Pte Ltd

MATH SHARING

SIMPLIFY IT FAST!

What you need:

Players: 2
Materials: Ratio cards

What to do:

1. Shuffle the cards and place the deck face down on the table.

2. Player 1 turns over the top card.

3. Both players shout out the equivalent ratio of the ratio on the card in simplest form. The faster player with the correct answer keeps the card.

4. Take turns to turn over the top card.

5. Play until all the cards have been won.

Who is the winner?

The player who collects more cards wins!

INDEPENDENT PRACTICE

Fill in each blank.

1. Ms. Jefferson has 3 boxes of yellow highlighters, 8 boxes of blue highlighters, and 7 boxes of orange highlighters. Each box contains 5 highlighters.

    a   The total number of _____ highlighters is 15.

    b   The total number of blue highlighters is _____.

    c   The ratio of the number of _____ highlighters to the number of

    blue highlighters is 15 : _____.

    d   The ratio of the number of boxes of yellow highlighters to the

    number of boxes of blue highlighters is _____ : 8.

    e   The ratios in **c** and **d** are _____.

    f   The ratio of the number of yellow highlighters to the number of

    orange highlighters is 3 : _____ or _____ : 35.

Express each ratio in simplest form.

2. 9 : 24 = _____ : _____

3. 16 : 10 = _____ : _____

4. 12 : 54 = _____ : _____

5. 56 : 32 = _____ : _____

Find the missing term in each set of equivalent ratios.

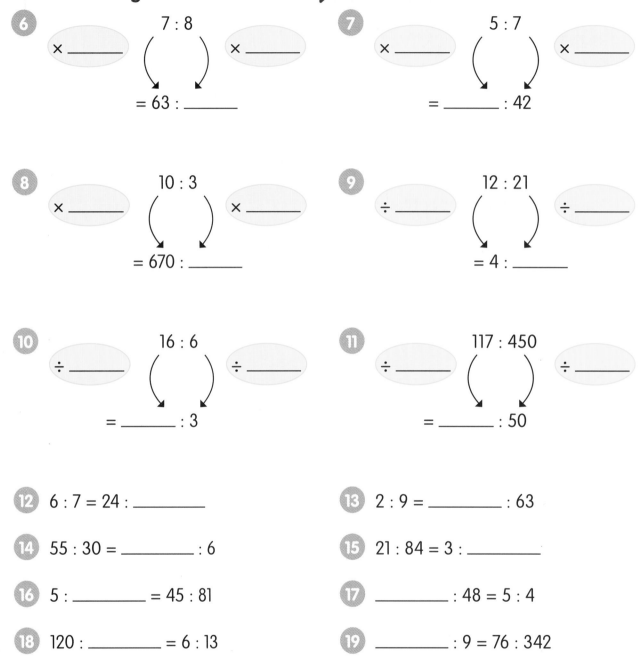

6.
× _____
7 : 8
× _____
= 63 : _____

7.
× _____
5 : 7
× _____
= _____ : 42

8.
× _____
10 : 3
× _____
= 670 : _____

9.
÷ _____
12 : 21
÷ _____
= 4 : _____

10.
÷ _____
16 : 6
÷ _____
= _____ : 3

11.
÷ _____
117 : 450
÷ _____
= _____ : 50

12. $6 : 7 = 24 :$ _____

13. $2 : 9 =$ _____ $: 63$

14. $55 : 30 =$ _____ $: 6$

15. $21 : 84 = 3 :$ _____

16. $5 :$ _____ $= 45 : 81$

17. _____ $: 48 = 5 : 4$

18. $120 :$ _____ $= 6 : 13$

19. _____ $: 9 = 76 : 342$

3 Comparing Three Quantities

Learning Objective:
• Read and write ratios of three quantities.

THINK

Jacob cuts a ribbon into three pieces. The first piece is twice as long as the second piece. The third piece is 4 times as long as the second piece.

a   Using a model, write a ratio of the length of the first piece to the length of the second piece to the length of the third piece.

b   Find two possible lengths of the original piece of ribbon.

ENGAGE

Gavin, Hailey, and Ian have a total of 24 baseball cards. Gavin has 8 baseball cards. What are the possible ratios of the number of baseball cards Gavin has to the number of baseball cards Hailey has to the number of baseball cards Ian has?

LEARN Express three quantities as a ratio

1   Rafael has 4 baseballs, 6 tennis balls and 8 ping pong balls.

The ratio of the number of baseballs to the number of tennis balls to the number of ping pong balls is 4 : 6 : 8.

He puts the balls into groups of 2.

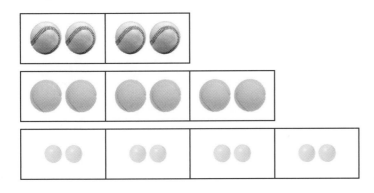

The ratio of the number of baseballs to the number of tennis balls to the number of ping pong balls is 2 : 3 : 4.

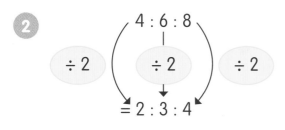

② $4 : 6 : 8$

$\div 2$ $\div 2$ $\div 2$

$= 2 : 3 : 4$

We divide the quantities by a common factor to express the ratio in simplest form.

So, 2 : 3 : 4 is the simplest form of 4 : 6 : 8.

Hands-on Activity Simplifying ratios

Work in pairs. Use 🎲.

① Count 8 🟦, 20 🟨, and 4 🟦.

② Ask your partner to write the ratio of the number of green cubes to the number of yellow cubes to the number of blue cubes.

③ Group each set of colored cubes separately such that there is an equal number of cubes in each group. Compare the number of groups to find an equivalent ratio.

④ Take turns to repeat ③ until all equivalent ratios are found. Which ratio is in simplest form?

⑤ Trade places. Repeat ① to ④ using 6 green cubes, 18 yellow cubes, and 24 blue cubes.

TRY Practice expressing three quantities as a ratio

Fill in each blank.

1) The ratio of the number of yellow cubes to the number of blue cubes to

the number of green cubes is 4 : _____ : _____.

2) The ratio of the number of yellow cubes to the number of blue cubes to

the number of green cubes is 2 : _____ : _____.

The ratio in its simplest form is _____ : _____ : _____.

Express each ratio in simplest form.

3) 5 : 15 : 20

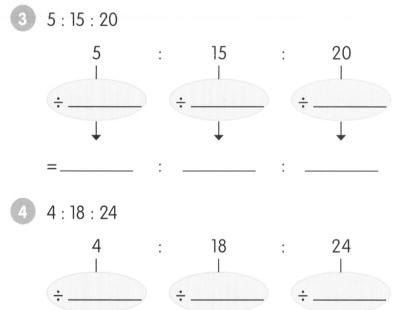

4) 4 : 18 : 24

$$\begin{array}{ccccc} 4 & : & 18 & : & 24 \\ | & & | & & | \\ \div\text{\_\_\_\_} & & \div\text{\_\_\_\_} & & \div\text{\_\_\_\_} \\ \downarrow & & \downarrow & & \downarrow \\ =\text{\_\_\_\_} & : & \text{\_\_\_\_} & : & \text{\_\_\_\_} \end{array}$$

5 15 : 12 : 18

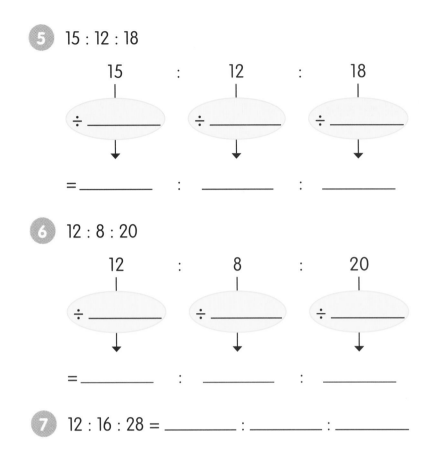

$$15 \quad : \quad 12 \quad : \quad 18$$

$\div$ _____ $\div$ _____ $\div$ _____

= _____ : _____ : _____

6 12 : 8 : 20

$$12 \quad : \quad 8 \quad : \quad 20$$

$\div$ _____ $\div$ _____ $\div$ _____

= _____ : _____ : _____

7 12 : 16 : 28 = _____ : _____ : _____

ENGAGE

Vijay cuts a stick into three pieces measuring of 2 feet, 3 feet, and 4 feet.
Julia cuts another stick in the same ratio. One of Julia's pieces is 18 feet.
What are the possible lengths of the other two pieces? Discuss with your partner.

LEARN Find an unknown value of an equivalent ratio

1 Find the missing numbers.
2 : 3 : 5 = ? : 12 : ?

▶ **Method 1**

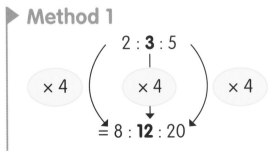

▶ **Method 2**

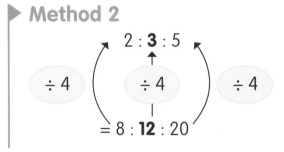

So, 2 : 3 : 5 = 8 : 12 : 20.

2 Find the missing numbers.

18 : 12 : 9 = ? : ? : 3

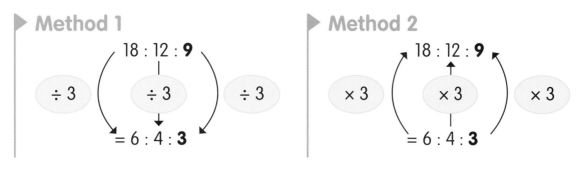

▶ **Method 1**

18 : 12 : **9**

÷ 3   ÷ 3   ÷ 3

= 6 : 4 : **3**

▶ **Method 2**

18 : 12 : **9**

× 3   × 3   × 3

= 6 : 4 : **3**

So, 18 : 12 : 9 = 6 : 4 : 3.

TRY Practice finding an unknown value of an equivalent ratio

Fill in each blank.

1 3 : 5 : 7 = 9 : ? : ?

3   :   5   :   7

× _____   × _____   × _____

=   9   :   _____   :   _____

2 1 : 4 : 5 = 3 : ? : ?

1   :   4   :   5

× _____   × _____   × _____

=   3   :   _____   :   _____

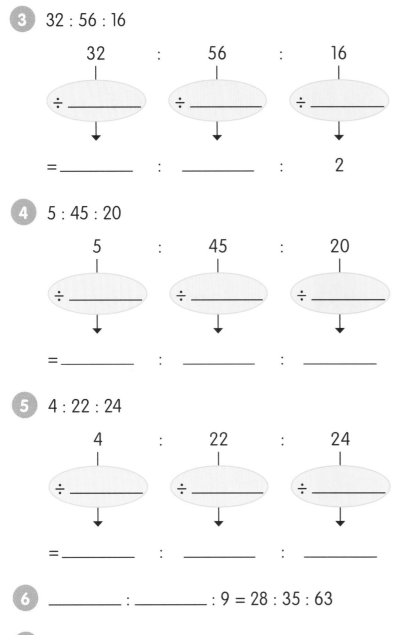

3 32 : 56 : 16

$$32 \quad : \quad 56 \quad : \quad 16$$

÷ _____   ÷ _____   ÷ _____

= _____ : _____ : 2

4 5 : 45 : 20

$$5 \quad : \quad 45 \quad : \quad 20$$

÷ _____   ÷ _____   ÷ _____

= _____ : _____ : _____

5 4 : 22 : 24

$$4 \quad : \quad 22 \quad : \quad 24$$

÷ _____   ÷ _____   ÷ _____

= _____ : _____ : _____

6 _____ : _____ : 9 = 28 : 35 : 63

7 _____ : _____ : 25 = 15 : 100 : 125

8 7 : 21 : 14 = _____ : _____ : 2

9 15 : 5 : 30 = _____ : 1 : _____

INDEPENDENT PRACTICE

Express each ratio in simplest form.

1 32 : 16 : 28

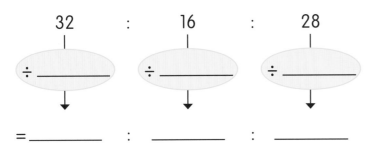

= _____ : _____ : _____

2 5 : 25 : 40

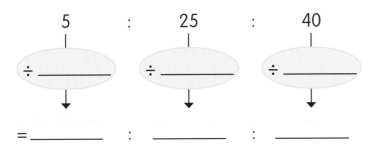

= _____ : _____ : _____

3 45 : 36 : 72

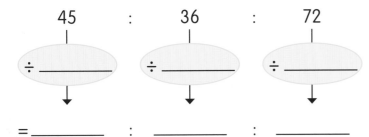

= _____ : _____ : _____

4 32 : 24 : 16

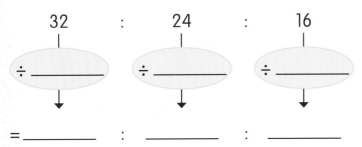

= _____ : _____ : _____

5 54 : 30 : 42

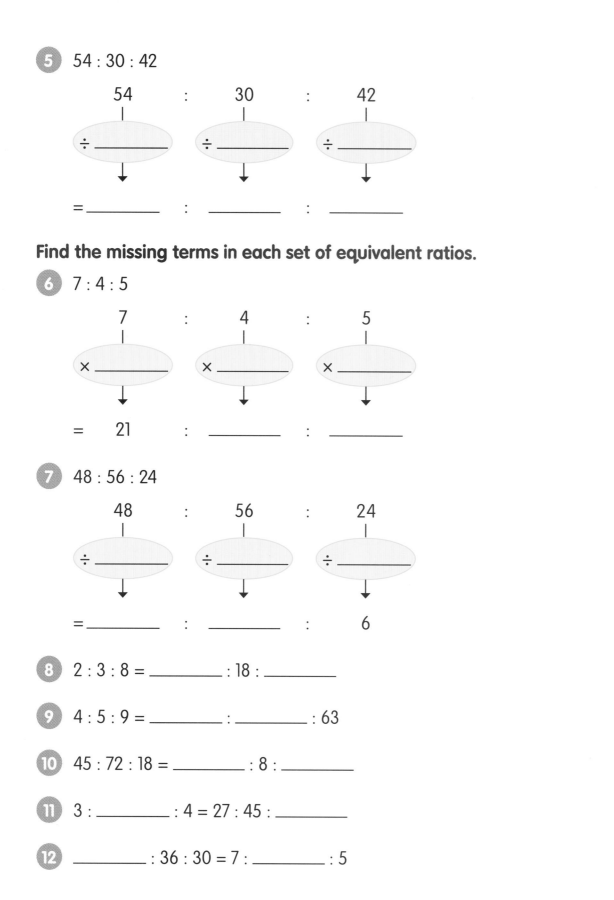

54 : 30 : 42

÷ _____   ÷ _____   ÷ _____

= _____ : _____ : _____

Find the missing terms in each set of equivalent ratios.

6 7 : 4 : 5

7 : 4 : 5

× _____   × _____   × _____

= 21 : _____ : _____

7 48 : 56 : 24

48 : 56 : 24

÷ _____   ÷ _____   ÷ _____

= _____ : _____ : 6

8 2 : 3 : 8 = _____ : 18 : _____

9 4 : 5 : 9 = _____ : _____ : 63

10 45 : 72 : 18 = _____ : 8 : _____

11 3 : _____ : 4 = 27 : 45 : _____

12 _____ : 36 : 30 = 7 : _____ : 5

4 Real-World Problems: Ratio

Learning Objective:
- Solve real-world problems involving ratio.

THINK

The ratio of the number of ripe apples to the number of unripe apples is 2 : 3.
The ratio of the number of ripe oranges to the number of unripe oranges is 3 : 7.
If the number of unripe apples is the same as the number of unripe oranges,
what is the least number of pieces of ripe fruit in all?

ENGAGE

39 fifth graders joined the art club or the drama club. If there are
15 fifth graders in the art club, what are some possible ratios to describe
the number of fifth graders in the art club to the number of fifth graders
in the drama club? Explain your reasoning.

LEARN Find ratios in simplest form to compare quantities in real-world problems

1. There are 6 angelfish and 18 tetras in an aquarium. Find the ratio
   of the number of angelfish to the number of tetras in the aquarium.
   Express the ratio in simplest form.

   The ratio of the number of angelfish to the number of tetras is 6 : 18.

   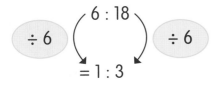

   Write the ratio 6 : 18 in simplest form. Divide 6 and 18 by their common factor 6.

   The ratio of the number of angelfish to the number of tetras in
   simplest form is 1 : 3.

2 Victoria had 10 pendants and 4 bracelets. Find the ratio of the number of pendants to the number of bracelets Victoria had. Express the ratio in simplest form.

Number of pendants : Number of bracelets

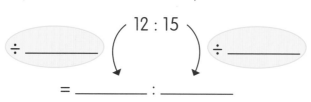

÷ 2 ⟨ 10 : 4 ⟩ ÷ 2
      5 : 2

The ratio of the number of pendants to the number of bracelets Victoria had was 5 : 2.

TRY Practice finding ratios in simplest form to compare quantities in real-world problems

Solve.

1 There are 12 pink roses and 15 yellow roses in Andre's garden. What is the ratio of
  a the number of pink roses to the number of yellow roses?
  b the number of yellow roses to the number of pink roses?
  Express each ratio in simplest form.

÷ _____ ⟨ 12 : 15 ⟩ ÷ _____

= _____ : _____

> Write the ratio 12 : 15 in simplest form. Divide 12 and 15 by the common factor, 3.

The ratio of the number of pink roses to the number of yellow roses is _____ : _____.

b The ratio of the number of yellow roses to the number of pink roses is _____ : _____.

2　Bruno baked 12 egg tarts, 15 muffins, and 24 cupcakes. Find the ratio of the number of egg tarts to the number of muffins to the number of cupcakes Bruno baked. Express the ratio in simplest form.

Number of egg tarts : Number of muffins : Number of cupcakes

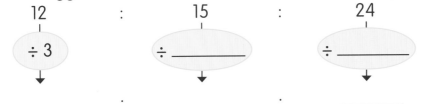

The ratio of the number of egg tarts to the number of muffins to the

number of cupcakes Bruno baked was _____ : _____ : _____.

3　There are 32 cats and 24 rabbits at an animal shelter. Write 2 ratio statements using the given data. Express each ratio in simplest form.

_____

_____

ENGAGE

There are 7 tables in a room. There are 3 times as many chairs as tables. Draw a model to find the number of chairs in the room.

LEARN Solve real-world problems involving ratios

1　There were 57 fifth and fourth graders in an art club. The ratio of the number of fifth graders to the number of fourth graders in the club was 1 : 2. How many fifth graders were there in the club?

STEP 1　Understand the problem.

How many students were in the club? What is the ratio of the number of fifth graders to the number of fourth graders? What do I need to find?

STEP 2　Think of a plan.
I can draw a bar model.

© 2020 Marshall Cavendish Education Pte Ltd

STEP 3 Carry out the plan.

fifth graders ▭
fourth graders ▭▭ } 57

3 units = 57
1 unit = 57 ÷ 3
= 19

There were 19 fifth graders in the club.

STEP 4 Check the answer.
I can work backwards to check my answer.

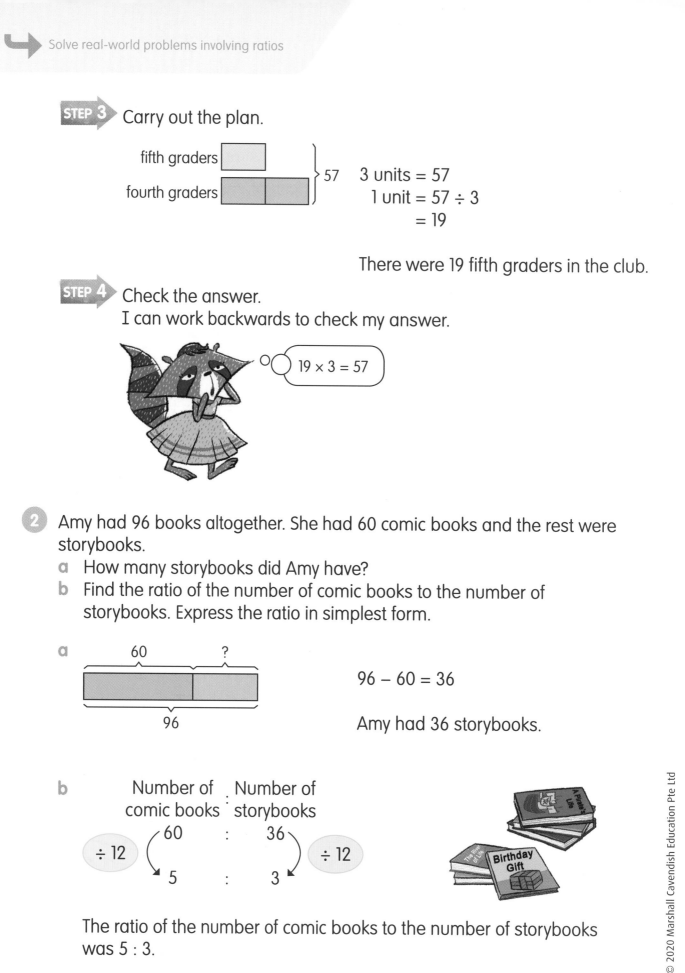

19 × 3 = 57

2 Amy had 96 books altogether. She had 60 comic books and the rest were storybooks.
  a How many storybooks did Amy have?
  b Find the ratio of the number of comic books to the number of storybooks. Express the ratio in simplest form.

a

60   ?

96

96 − 60 = 36

Amy had 36 storybooks.

b

Number of   Number of
comic books : storybooks

÷ 12 (60 : 36) ÷ 12

5 : 3

The ratio of the number of comic books to the number of storybooks was 5 : 3.

3 Sofia divides a carton of tomatoes into two portions. The ratio of the mass of the bigger portion to the mass of the smaller portion is 5 : 2. The mass of the bigger portion is 15 pounds. Find the mass of the smaller portion.

▶ **Method 1**

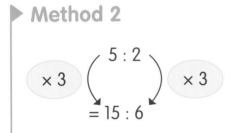

5 units = 15 lb
 1 unit = 15 ÷ 5
         = 3 lb
2 units = 2 × 3
         = 6 lb

The mass of the smaller portion of tomatoes is 6 pounds.

▶ **Method 2**

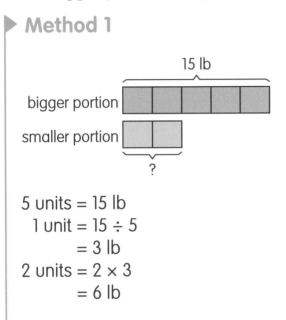

$5 \times 3 = 15$
$2 \times 3 = 6$

The mass of the smaller portion of tomatoes is 6 pounds.

4 There were peach, pear, and apple trees in an orchard. The ratio of the number of peach trees to the number of pear trees to the number of apple trees was 3 : 2 : 4. There were 24 peach trees.
a How many more apple trees were there than pear trees?
b How many fruit trees were there altogether in the orchard?

a

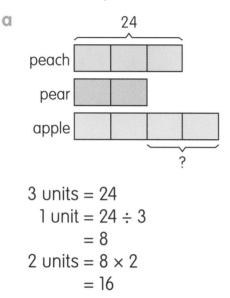

3 units = 24
  1 unit = 24 ÷ 3
        = 8
2 units = 8 × 2
        = 16

There were 16 more apple trees than pear trees.

b 3 + 2 + 4 = 9
9 units = 8 × 9
        = 72

There were 72 fruit trees altogether in the orchard.

5 Mr. Davis spent some of his monthly salary on food and gas and saved the rest. The ratio of the amount of money spent on food to the amount of money spent on gas to the amount of money saved was 2 : 3 : 5. The amount Mr. Davis saved was $480 more than the amount he spent on gas. How much money did he save?

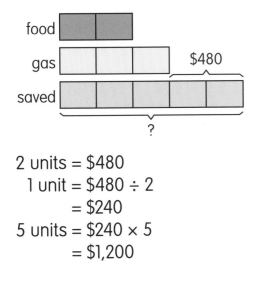

2 units = $480
  1 unit = $480 ÷ 2
        = $240
5 units = $240 × 5
        = $1,200

He saved $1,200.

Hands-on Activity Using models to solve real-world problems

Activity 1 Drawing part-whole models to solve problems

Work in pairs.

① Read the word problem. Draw a bar model for the problem.

Zoe used 125 centimeters of ribbon to tie a present and had 75 centimeters of ribbon left. Find the ratio of the length of ribbon she used to the length of the ribbon she had at first. Express the ratio in simplest form.

2 Ask your partner to use your bar model to solve the problem.

3 Check your partner's answer in **2**.

4 Trade places. Repeat **1** to **3** for the following word problems.

a A box contained 56 apples. 18 of the apples were green and the rest were red. Find the ratio of the number of red apples to the number of green apples. Express the ratio in simplest form.

b Nicolás mixed 300 milliliters of cranberry juice with 200 milliliters of water. He then added another 150 milliliters of water. Find the amount of cranberry juice to the amount of water in the end. Express the ratio in simplest form.

c A baker baked 120 chicken pies, 200 meat pies, and 160 tuna pies. Express the ratio of the number of chicken pies to the number of meat pies to the number of tuna pies in simplest form.

Activity 2   Drawing comparison models to solve problems

Work in pairs.

1. Read the word problem. Draw a bar model for the problem.

    Stephanie and Miguel divided some beads in the ratio 7 : 5. Miguel's share was 30 beads. How many beads did Stephanie have?

2. Ask your partner to use your bar model to solve the problem.

3. Check your partner's answer in ②.

4. Trade places. Repeat ① to ③ for the following word problems.

    a   The ratio of the number of visitors to a museum in the morning to the number of visitors in the afternoon was 3 : 5. There was a total of 216 visitors. How many visitors were there in the afternoon?

b A fruit stall had apples, pears, and oranges in the ratio 3 : 1 : 4. There were 720 apples. How many pieces of fruit were there in all?

c The number of red roses, yellow roses, and pink roses at a florist are in the ratio 5 : 2 : 6. There are 36 more red roses than yellow roses. How many pink roses are there?

TRY Practice solving real-world problems involving ratios

Solve. Use the bar model to help you.

1. Tomas and Jayla ran a total of 1,000 meters. The ratio of the distance Tomas ran to the distance Jayla ran was 1 : 4. What was the distance Tomas ran?

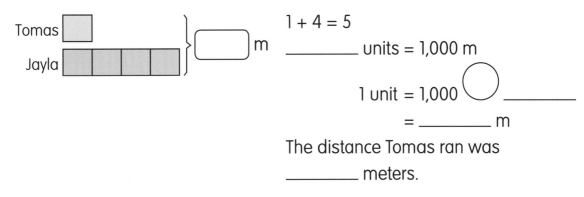

1 + 4 = 5

_____ units = 1,000 m

1 unit = 1,000 ◯ _____

= _____ m

The distance Tomas ran was

_____ meters.

2 Mr. Hall gave his 3 children 900 basketball cards to share among themselves. Zoe received 200 cards, Dylan received 400 cards, and Luke received the remaining cards.

a How many cards did Luke receive?

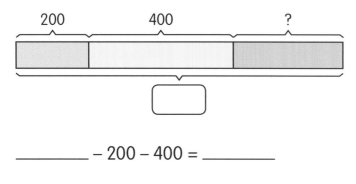

_____ – 200 – 400 = _____

Luke received _____ cards.

b Find the ratio of the number of cards Zoe received to the number Dylan received to the number Luke received. Express the ratio in simplest form.

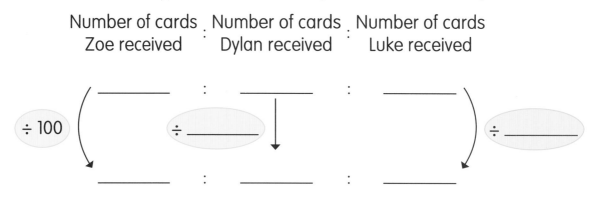

The ratio of the number of cards Zoe received to the number Dylan

received to the number Luke received was _____ : _____ : _____ .

3 Ms. Lewis had some flour. She used 800 grams of it to bake a cake and the rest of it to bake a loaf of bread. The ratio of the mass of flour used for the cake to the mass of flour used for the loaf of bread was 4 : 5. How much flour did Ms. Lewis use to bake the loaf of bread?

▶ **Method 1**

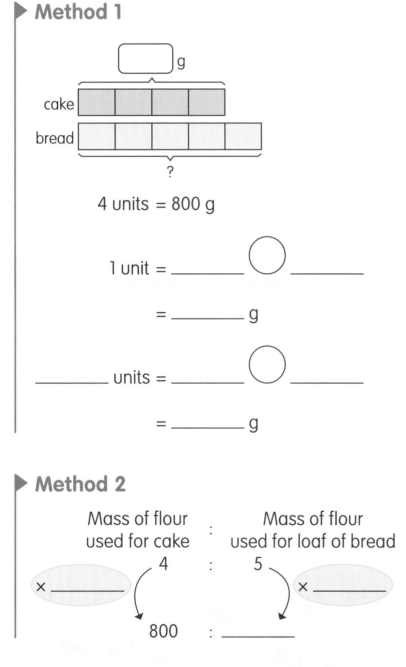

4 units = 800 g

1 unit = _____ ◯ _____

= _____ g

_____ units = _____ ◯ _____

= _____ g

▶ **Method 2**

Mass of flour used for cake : Mass of flour used for loaf of bread

4 : 5

× _____ (800 : _____) × _____

Ms. Lewis used _____ grams of flour to bake the loaf of bread.

4 At a carnival, the number of adult visitors to the number of crew members to the number of children is 4 : 7 : 9. There are 26 more children than crew members. How many adult visitors are there at the carnival?

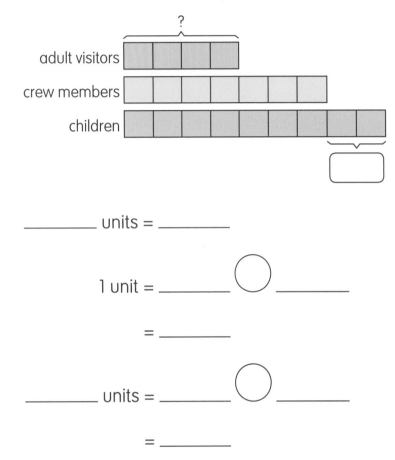

_____ units = _____

1 unit = _____ ◯ _____

= _____

_____ units = _____ ◯ _____

= _____

There are _____ adult visitors at the carnival.

INDEPENDENT PRACTICE

Solve. Draw a bar model to help you.

1 Mr. Clark spent $27 on a pair of shoes and $18 on a shirt. Find the ratio of the amount of money spent on the pair of shoes to the shirt. Express the ratio in simplest form.

2 A bag contained 32 puffs. 14 had custard filling and the rest had cheese filling. Find the ratio of the number of custard puffs to the number of cheese puffs. Express the ratio in simplest form.

3 Logan mixed 500 milliliters of cranberry juice, 600 milliliters of grapefruit juice, and 1 liter of water to make fruit punch. What was the ratio of the amount of cranberry juice to grapefruit juice to water he used? Express the ratio in simplest form.

4　Linus bought 12 assessment books, 30 folders, and 48 color pencils. What was the ratio of the number of assessment books to the number of folders to the number of color pencils he bought? Express the ratio in simplest form.

5　Aika spent a total of 80 minutes to complete her math and science homework. The ratio of the amount of time she spent to complete her science homework to the amount of time she spent to complete her math homework was 3 : 2. How many minutes did she spend on her math homework?

© 2020 Marshall Cavendish Education Pte Ltd

6 Silas lost 11 pounds in a year after joining the basketball team and now weighs 88 pounds. Find the ratio of his current weight to his weight before he joined the basketball team. Express the ratio in simplest form.

7 There were 18 cows and 23 goats on a farm. The farm bought another 3 cows and 5 goats. Find the ratio of the number of cows to the number of goats on the farm in the end. Express the ratio in simplest form.

8 Mr. Thomas cuts a coil of wire into two pieces in the ratio 3 : 4. The length of the longer piece of wire is 32 centimeters. What is the original length of the coil of wire?

9 Kalini mixed some apple, carrot, and celery juices. The ratio of the amount of apple juice to the amount of carrot juice to the amount of celery juice was 2 : 3 : 7. The total amount of juice was 1,200 milliliters. How many milliliters of celery juice were used?

10. Richard draws three lines in the colors red, yellow and green. The ratio of the length of the red line to the length of the yellow line to the length of the green line is 1 : 3 : 5. The yellow line is 18 inches long. How long is the green line?

11. On Sunday, the ratio of the number of customers at a furniture store in the morning to the number of customers in the afternoon to the number of customers in the evening was 3 : 5 : 9. There were 219 customers in the morning. What was the total number of customers at the furniture store on Sunday?

12 Issac is 5 years older than Trevon. The ratio of Issac's age to Trevon's age is 4 : 3. How old is Trevon?

13 The masses of three bags, A, B, and C are in the ratio 6 : 4 : 5. The difference between the mass of bag B and the mass of bag C is 3 kilograms. Find the mass of bag A.

Mathematical Habit 4 Use mathematical models

1 Look at the bar model.
Write a real-world problem that includes a ratio. Then, solve your real-world problem.

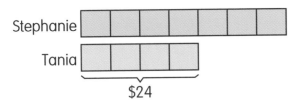

Stephanie

Tania

$24

2 Daniel said that the question below cannot be solved. Do you agree?
Explain.
12 : 16 = 9 : _____

Problem Solving with Heuristics

1 **Mathematical Habit 4** Use mathematical models

Ms. Lopez has some $2 bills and $10 bills. The ratio of the value of the $2 bills to the value of the $10 bills is 3 : 5. Find the least number of $2 bills.

2 **Mathematical Habit 4** Use mathematical models

There are some motorcycles and cars in a garage. The ratio of the total number of motorcycle wheels to the total number of car wheels is 2 : 9. Find the least number of motorcycles in the garage.

3 **Mathematical Habit 8** Look for patterns

Look at the pattern.

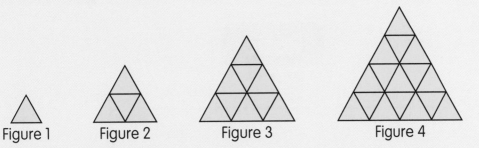

Figure 1   Figure 2   Figure 3   Figure 4   ?   Figure 5

What is the ratio of the area of Figure 1 to the area of Figure 5?

CHAPTER WRAP-UP

How can you relate and compare two or three quantities?

Ratio

Comparing Numbers or Quantities

Equivalent Ratios

- Ratios can be used to compare two or three quantities.
- A ratio may not give the actual quantities compared.
- A ratio has no units.

- Multiply by a common factor to find equivalent ratios.

$\times 3$ 1 : 3 $\times 3$
       3 : 9

4 : 7 : 9
$\times 4$ $\times 4$ $\times 4$
16 : 28 : 36

- Divide by a common factor to find equivalent ratios.

$\div 2$ 10 : 8 $\div 2$
       5 : 4

24 : 40 : 16
$\div 8$ $\div 8$ $\div 8$
3 : 5 : 2

5 : 4 is the simplest form of 10 : 8.

3 : 5 : 2 is the simplest form of 24 : 40 : 16.

Fill in each blank. Write each ratio in simplest form.

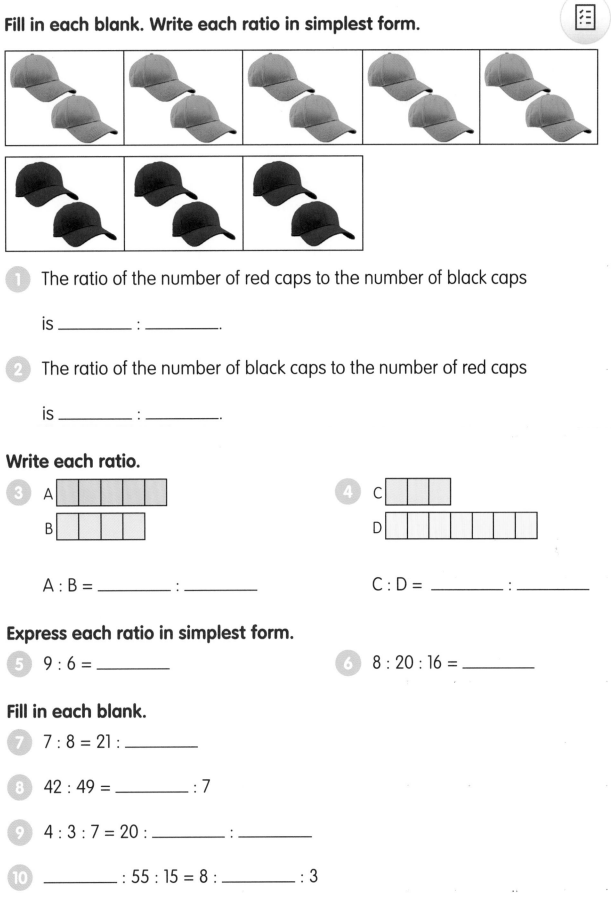

① The ratio of the number of red caps to the number of black caps

is _____ : _____.

② The ratio of the number of black caps to the number of red caps

is _____ : _____.

Write each ratio.

③ A B

A : B = _____ : _____

④ C D

C : D = _____ : _____

Express each ratio in simplest form.

⑤ 9 : 6 = _____

⑥ 8 : 20 : 16 = _____

Fill in each blank.

⑦ 7 : 8 = 21 : _____

⑧ 42 : 49 = _____ : 7

⑨ 4 : 3 : 7 = 20 : _____ : _____

⑩ _____ : 55 : 15 = 8 : _____ : 3

Solve. Draw a bar model to help you.

11 Madison cut a 2-meter roll of ribbon into three pieces, A, B, and C. The ratio of the lengths of A, B, and C was 5 : 2 : 1. Find the length of the longest piece of ribbon in centimeters.

12 The ratio of the perimeter of a square piece of paper to the perimeter of a rectangular piece of paper is 2 : 5. The square piece of paper has sides 10 centimeters. Find the perimeter of the rectangular piece of paper.

13 Ms. Cooper bought some erasers, pens, and pencils. The ratio of the number of erasers to the number of pens to the number of pencils was 1 : 3 : 8. She bought 60 items altogether. How many pencils did Ms. Cooper buy?

14. The ratio of the number of football cards Adrián, Brandon, and Chloe had was 2 : 3 : 15. Chloe had 1,575 football cards. What was the total number of football cards Adrián, Brandon, and Chloe had?

15. A baker sold muffins, bagels, and flatbreads in the ratio 12 : 5 : 7. The number of muffins sold was 50 more than the number of flatbreads sold. How many muffins did the baker sell?

Assessment Prep

Answer each question.

16 What is the ratio of the number of apples to the number of oranges in simplest form?

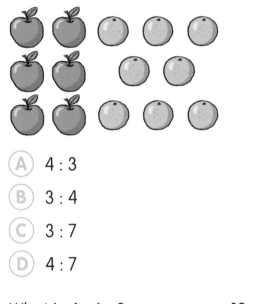

Ⓐ 4 : 3

Ⓑ 3 : 4

Ⓒ 3 : 7

Ⓓ 4 : 7

17 What is 4 : 6 : 9 = _____ : 18 : _____?
Write your answer in the space below.

18 Elijah had 12 colored pencils, 4 pens, and 8 pencils. He wrote the ratio of the number of colored pencils to pens to pencils in simplest form as 6 : 2 : 4.
 • Do you agree with Elijah?
 • Explain your reasoning.

Write your answer and explanation in the space below.

Office Supplies

1 Andrew and Tiana design a poster to advertise their school's charity bake sale. They draw the design on a sheet of paper that measures 9 inches wide and 12 inches long. They go to an office supply store to make copies of their poster to put up around the school.

a What is the ratio of the width of their original drawing to its length? Express the ratio in simplest form. Draw a diagram and explain your answer.

b The children want to enlarge their drawing to print a banner that is 60 inches long. If the ratio of the width to the length of the banner is the same as the original drawing, what will the width of the banner be? Draw a diagram and explain your answer.

2 The children decide to have fliers, banners, and posters printed for the bake sale in a ratio of 25 : 1 : 3. They print 200 fliers.

a How many fliers, banners, and posters do the children print in all? Draw a bar model and explain your answer.

b How many more fliers than posters do the boys print? Use your bar model in a and explain your answer.

3 While at the office supply store, the children buy rolls of tape to use to put up the posters around the school. Andrew buys $\frac{2}{7}$ times the number of rolls of tape that Tony buys. If Tony buys 21 rolls of tape, how many rolls of tape do the boys buy in all? Draw a bar model and explain your answer.

Rubric

Point(s)	Level	My Performance
7–8	4	• Most of my answers are correct. • I showed complete understanding of what I have learned. • I used the correct strategies to solve the problems. • I explained my answers and mathematical thinking clearly and completely.
5–6.5	3	• Some of my answers are correct. • I showed some understanding of what I have learned. • I used some correct strategies to solve the problems. • I explained my answers and mathematical thinking clearly.
3–4.5	2	• A few of my answers are correct. • I showed little understanding of what I have learned. • I used a few correct strategies to solve the problems. • I explained some of my answers and mathematical thinking clearly.
0–2.5	1	• A few of my answers are correct. • I showed little or no understanding of what I have learned. • I used a few strategies to solve the problems. • I did not explain my answers and mathematical thinking clearly.

Teacher's Comments

STEAM

MPG

The expression "miles per gallon," or mpg, describes the distance a car can travel on one gallon of gas. It is a measure of fuel efficiency. A fuel-efficient car has a higher mpg rating. It uses less gas to go farther.

Task

The Cost of a Field Trip

Work in pairs or small groups to calculate the cost of a field trip.

1 Imagine you can go anywhere on a class field trip. The only rule is that the class must travel by car.

2 Go to the library or go online to:
- read about cars and fuel efficiency. Choose a car that will carry at least 5 people, including an adult driver. Record the car's fuel efficiency.
- find the most direct driving route to your field-trip destination. Record the round-trip distance to the nearest mile.
- find the cost of a gallon of gasoline.

3 Calculate how many cars you will need. Then figure out how many gallons of gasoline each driver will need to make one complete round trip. Finally, find the total gasoline cost for the class.

4 Compare field-trip destinations, cars, and gasoline costs.

5 Imagine you are on the trip you planned and you are having a great time. You are taking self-portrait photographs and sending text messages to your families back home. Write some of the text messages you are sending describing your experience. Add your text messages to a Class Field Trip message board.

Chapter 10 Percent

What does percent mean? How can you represent a percent in different ways? How can percents be used in real-world situations?

Name: _____ Date: _____

Writing fractions with a denominator of 100 as a decimal

$\frac{37}{100}$ of the square is shaded.

$\frac{37}{100}$ can be written as 0.37.

0.37 is the same as $\frac{37}{100}$ or 37 out of 100.

▶ Quick Check

Express as a decimal.

1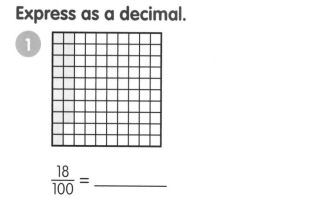

$\frac{18}{100}$ = _____

2

$\frac{65}{100}$ = _____

Express as a fraction with a denominator of 100.

3 24 out of 100 _____

4 53 out of 100 _____

Fill in each blank.

5 $\frac{13}{100}$ is ____ out of ____.

6 $\frac{21}{100}$ is ____ out of ____.

7 0.97 is ____ out of ____.

8 0.73 is ____ out of ____.

Finding equivalent fractions using multiplication

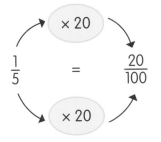

$$\frac{1}{5} = \frac{20}{100}$$

▶ **Quick Check**

Fill in each blank.

9 $\dfrac{3}{5} = \dfrac{6}{\boxed{}} = \dfrac{\boxed{}}{100}$

10 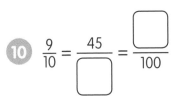 $\dfrac{9}{10} = \dfrac{45}{\boxed{}} = \dfrac{\boxed{}}{100}$

11 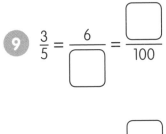 $\dfrac{3}{4} = \dfrac{6}{\boxed{}} = \dfrac{\boxed{}}{100}$

12 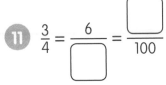 $\dfrac{4}{5} = \dfrac{\boxed{}}{20} = \dfrac{\boxed{}}{100}$

Simplifying fractions using division

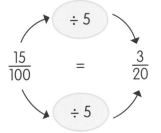

$$\frac{15}{100} = \frac{3}{20}$$

▶ **Quick Check**

Express each fraction in simplest form.

13 $\dfrac{15}{25} = \dfrac{\boxed{}}{\boxed{}}$

14 $\dfrac{35}{100} = \dfrac{\boxed{}}{\boxed{}}$

Finding equivalent fractions and decimals

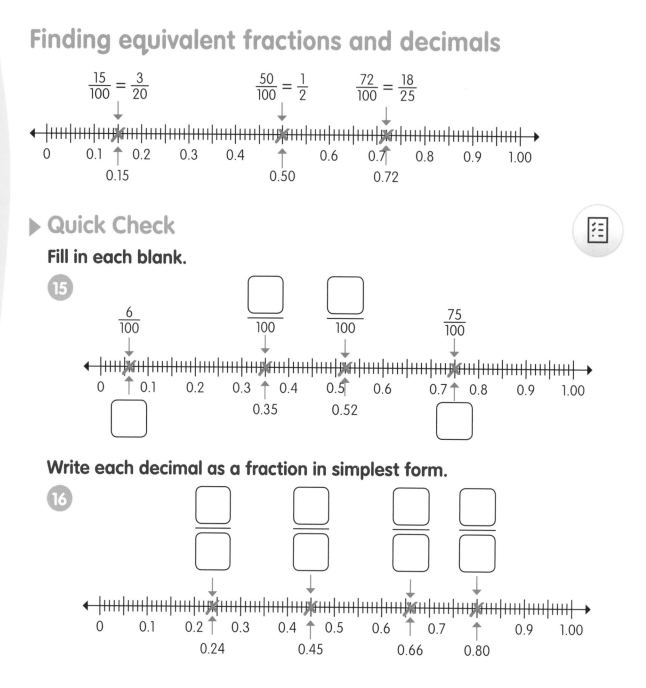

$$\frac{15}{100} = \frac{3}{20} \qquad \frac{50}{100} = \frac{1}{2} \qquad \frac{72}{100} = \frac{18}{25}$$

▶ **Quick Check**

Fill in each blank.

15

Write each decimal as a fraction in simplest form.

16

1 Percent

Learning Objective:
• Relate a percent to parts of a whole where the whole is made up of 100 equal parts.

THINK

Ethan has 2 green apples and 6 red apples.
a   What fraction of the apples are red?
b   How many red apples must be replaced with green apples so that each type of apple is 50% of the whole?

ENGAGE

Megan shaded some squares on a 100-square grid as shown.
How can you express the shaded parts in different ways? Explain to your partner.

LEARN Use a percent to represent part of a whole

1

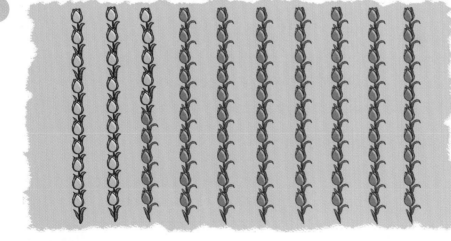

There are 100 tulips.
75 of them are red.
So, 75 out of 100 tulips are red.
75 out of 100 can be represented as 75%.

The symbol for percent is %.
You read 75% as seventy-five percent.

2 Divide each square into 100 equal parts.

1 out of 100 parts is shaded.

$\frac{1}{100}$ of the whole is shaded.

1% of the whole is shaded.

99% of the whole is **not** shaded.

$1\% = \frac{1}{100}$
$= 0.01$

64 out of 100 parts are shaded.

$\frac{64}{100}$ of the whole is shaded.

64% of the whole is shaded.

36% of the whole is **not** shaded.

1%, 99%, 64%, and 36% are percents.

Any number can be written as a part of 100 or a percent.

TRY Practice using a percent to represent part of a whole

Fill in each blank.

1

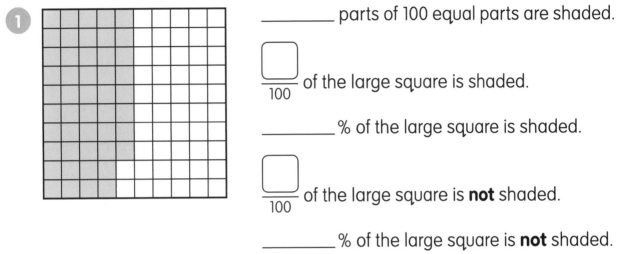

_____ parts of 100 equal parts are shaded.

$\dfrac{\boxed{}}{100}$ of the large square is shaded.

_____ % of the large square is shaded.

$\dfrac{\boxed{}}{100}$ of the large square is **not** shaded.

_____ % of the large square is **not** shaded.

In each figure, write the shaded parts as a percent of the whole figure.

2

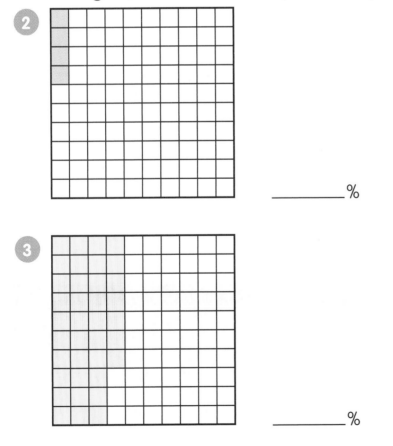

_____ %

3

_____ %

4

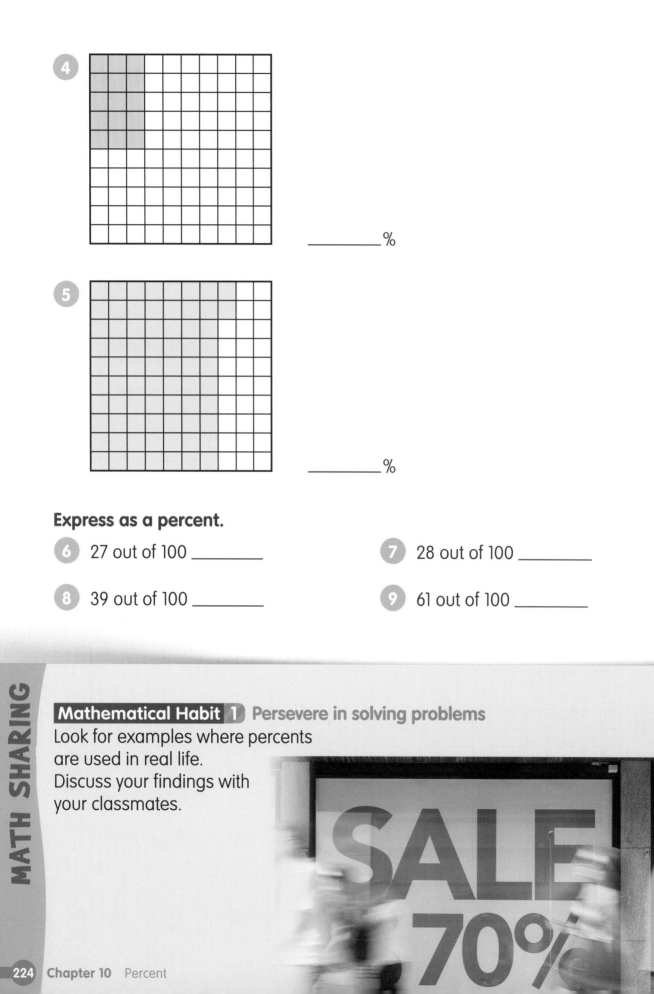

_____ %

5

_____ %

Express as a percent.

6 27 out of 100 _____

7 28 out of 100 _____

8 39 out of 100 _____

9 61 out of 100 _____

SALE
70%

© 2020 Marshall Cavendish Education Pte Ltd

INDEPENDENT PRACTICE

In each figure, write the shaded parts as a percent of the whole figure.

1

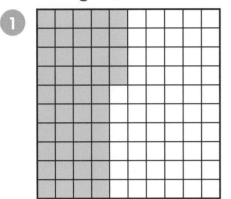

_____

2

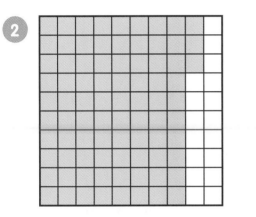

_____

Fill in each blank.

3

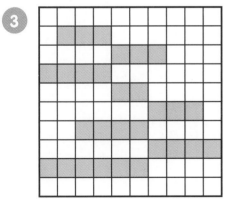

_____% of the whole figure is shaded.

_____% of the whole figure is **not** shaded.

Shade 63% of the whole figure.

4

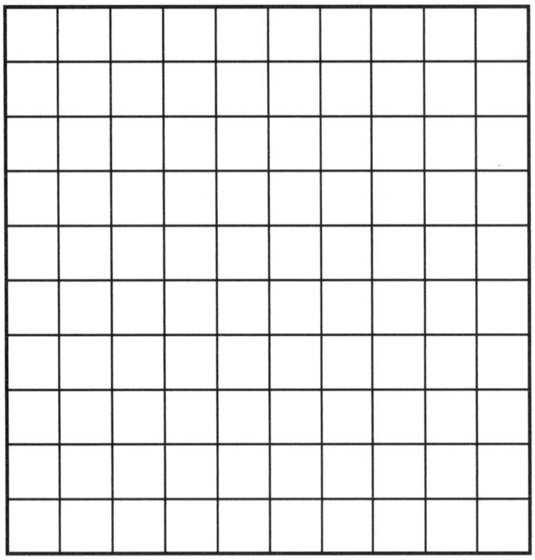

Express as a percent.

5 49 out of 100 = _____ %

6 91 out of 100 = _____ %

7 _____ out of 100 = 30%

8 _____ out of 100 = 7%

2 Fractions, Decimals, and Percents

Learning Objectives:
- Relate and compare percents, decimals, and fractions.
- Express fractions as percents and vice versa.
- Express decimals as percents and vice versa.

THINK

Alexa wrote 4% as 0.4 and Tiana wrote 4% as $\frac{40}{100}$. Who is correct? Explain.

ENGAGE

Marco wants to shade 55% of a 100-square grid. He shades the grid as shown. Is he correct? How do you know? Use fractions or decimals to explain your thinking.

LEARN Write percents as fractions and decimals

1 Express 60% as a fraction.

▶ **Method 1**

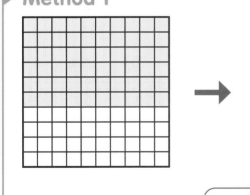

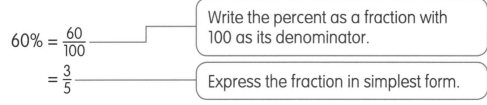

$60\% = \frac{60}{100}$ —— Write the percent as a fraction with 100 as its denominator.

$= \frac{3}{5}$ —— Express the fraction in simplest form.

Method 2

A diagram can be used to express a percent as a fraction.

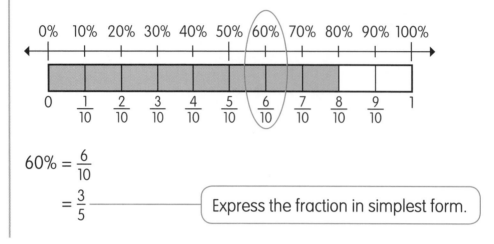

$60\% = \dfrac{6}{10}$

$\quad\; = \dfrac{3}{5}$ ——————— Express the fraction in simplest form.

2 Express 45% as a decimal.

Method 1

$45\% = \dfrac{45}{100}$

$\quad\;\; = 0.45$

Method 2

A number line can be used to express a percent as a decimal.

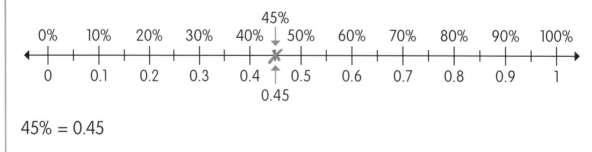

$45\% = 0.45$

Activity 1   Show the relationship between a percent and a fraction

Work in pairs.

1. Draw a diagram and shade the parts to show 80%.
   a   How many parts make up a whole?
   b   How many parts are shaded?

2. Ask your partner to express 80% as a fraction in simplest form.

3. Trade places. Repeat ① and ② with 25%.

Activity 2 Show the relationship between a percent and a decimal

Work in pairs.

1. Draw a number line with intervals of 10% and mark a cross to show 45%.

2. Ask your partner to express 45% as a decimal. Your partner labels each decimal interval on the number line in ①, then labels 45% expressed as a decimal.

3. Trade places. Repeat ① and ② with 75%.

TRY Practice writing percents as fractions and decimals

Express 64% as a fraction in simplest form.

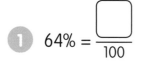

1. $64\% = \dfrac{\boxed{}}{100}$

   $= \rule{2cm}{0.4pt}$

Express each percent as a fraction in simplest form.

2. 70%

3. 5%

4. 94%

5. 50%

6. 12%

7. 75%

Express 81% as a decimal.

8. 81% = $\dfrac{\boxed{}}{100}$

= _____

Express each percent as a decimal.

9. 39%

10. 91%

11. 9%

12. 20%

ENGAGE

a Michael spent $\frac{1}{4}$ of his lunch break at the library. What percent of his lunch break did he spend at the library?

b If his lunch break was 40 minutes, how many minutes was he at the library? Discuss with your partner two different ways to find the answer.

LEARN Write fractions and decimals as percents

1 Express 0.7 as a percent.

▶ **Method 1**

$$0.7 = \frac{7}{10}$$
$$= \frac{70}{100}$$ —— The denominator must be 100.
$$= 70\%$$

▶ **Method 2**

A number line can be used to express a decimal as a percent.

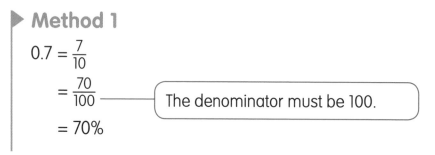

0.7 = 70%

▶ **Method 3**

Multiply by 100%.
$$0.7 = 0.7 \times 100\%$$
$$= 70\%$$

2 Express $\frac{1}{4}$ as a percent.

▶ **Method 1**

$\frac{1}{4} = \frac{25}{100}$ ── Express as a fraction with 100 as the denominator.

$\qquad = 25\%$

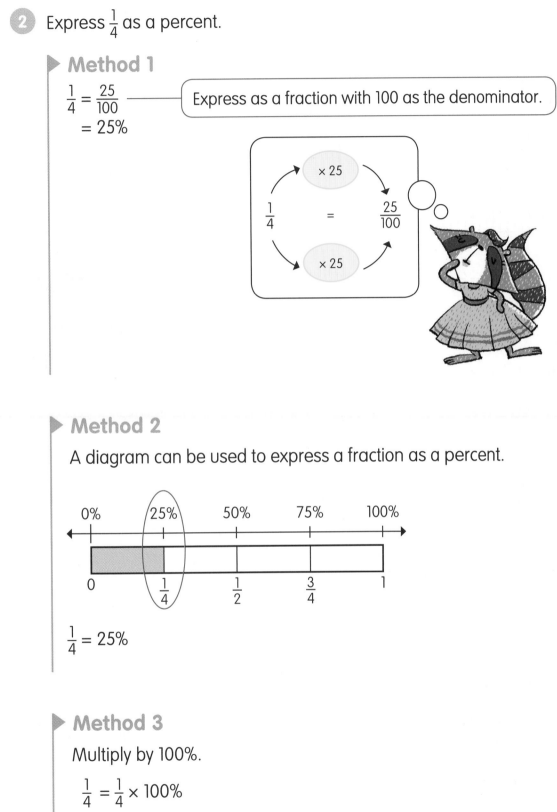

▶ **Method 2**

A diagram can be used to express a fraction as a percent.

$\frac{1}{4} = 25\%$

▶ **Method 3**

Multiply by 100%.

$\frac{1}{4} = \frac{1}{4} \times 100\%$

$\qquad = 25\%$

3 Express $\frac{120}{200}$ as a percent.

▶ **Method 1**

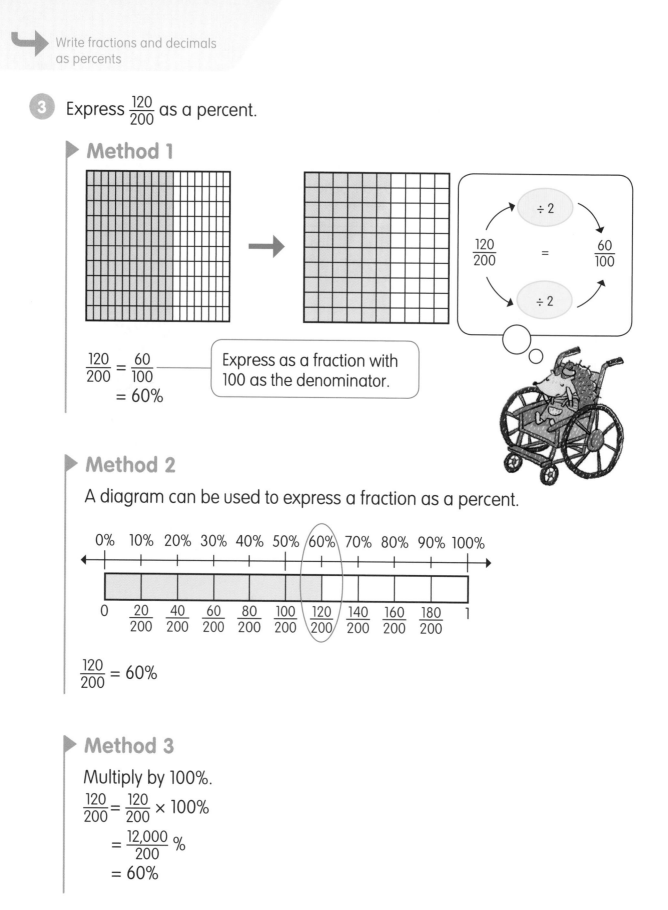

$\frac{120}{200} = \frac{60}{100}$ ——— Express as a fraction with 100 as the denominator.

$= 60\%$

▶ **Method 2**

A diagram can be used to express a fraction as a percent.

0% 10% 20% 30% 40% 50% 60% 70% 80% 90% 100%

0   $\frac{20}{200}$ $\frac{40}{200}$ $\frac{60}{200}$ $\frac{80}{200}$ $\frac{100}{200}$ $\frac{120}{200}$ $\frac{140}{200}$ $\frac{160}{200}$ $\frac{180}{200}$ 1

$\frac{120}{200} = 60\%$

▶ **Method 3**

Multiply by 100%.

$\frac{120}{200} = \frac{120}{200} \times 100\%$

$= \frac{12,000}{200}\%$

$= 60\%$

④ Express $\frac{3}{8}$ as a percent.

$\frac{3}{8} = 3 \div 8 \times 100\%$

$\quad = 0.375 \times 100\%$

$\quad = 37.5\%$

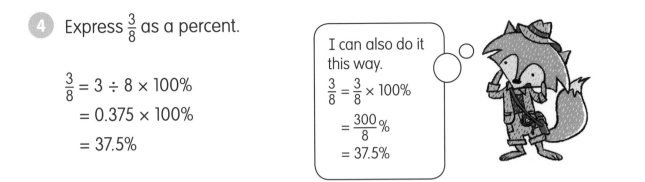

I can also do it this way.

$\frac{3}{8} = \frac{3}{8} \times 100\%$

$\quad = \frac{300}{8}\%$

$\quad = 37.5\%$

Hands-on Activity Express a part of a whole as a percent

Work in pairs.

① Shade the parts in the 100-square grid to show 30%. How many parts out of 100 are shaded?

② Ask your partner to shade the parts on the 200-part grid to show 30%. How many parts out of 200 are shaded?

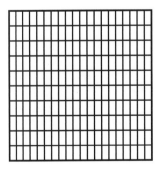

③ What do you notice?

TRY Practice writing fractions and decimals as percents

Fill in each blank. Express each decimal as a percent.

1 $0.56 = \dfrac{\boxed{}}{100}$

   $= \underline{\hspace{2cm}} \%$

2 $0.08 = \underline{\hspace{2cm}}$

   $= \underline{\hspace{2cm}} \%$

Express each decimal as a percent.

3 0.03

4 0.07

5 0.4

6 0.9

7 0.46

8 0.91

9 0.22

10 0.64

11 0.15

12 0.78

Fill in each blank. Express each fraction as a percent.

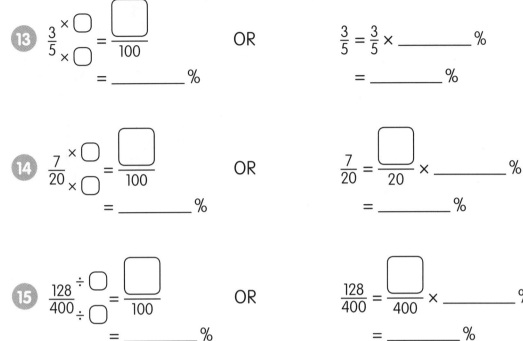

13 $\dfrac{3}{5} \begin{matrix} \times\ \bigcirc \\ \times\ \bigcirc \end{matrix} = \dfrac{\boxed{}}{100}$ **OR** $\dfrac{3}{5} = \dfrac{3}{5} \times \underline{\hspace{2cm}}\ \%$

       $= \underline{\hspace{2cm}}\ \%$ $= \underline{\hspace{2cm}}\ \%$

14 $\dfrac{7}{20} \begin{matrix} \times\ \bigcirc \\ \times\ \bigcirc \end{matrix} = \dfrac{\boxed{}}{100}$ **OR** $\dfrac{7}{20} = \dfrac{\boxed{}}{20} \times \underline{\hspace{2cm}}\ \%$

       $= \underline{\hspace{2cm}}\ \%$ $= \underline{\hspace{2cm}}\ \%$

15 $\dfrac{128}{400} \begin{matrix} \div\ \bigcirc \\ \div\ \bigcirc \end{matrix} = \dfrac{\boxed{}}{100}$ **OR** $\dfrac{128}{400} = \dfrac{\boxed{}}{400} \times \underline{\hspace{2cm}}\ \%$

       $= \underline{\hspace{2cm}}\ \%$ $= \underline{\hspace{2cm}}\ \%$

Express each fraction as a percent.

16 $\dfrac{9}{10}$ 17 $\dfrac{11}{20}$

18 $\dfrac{12}{25}$ 19 $\dfrac{21}{300}$

20 $\dfrac{7}{8}$ 21 $\dfrac{3}{150}$

PAIR THEM UP!

What you need:

Players: 4
Materials: Percent cards

What to do:

1. Shuffle the deck of cards and distribute five cards to each player. Place the remaining cards face down to form a DRAW pile.

2. At the start of a turn, Player 1 draws a card from the DRAW pile. He or she finds as many matching cards as possible in his or her hands, then puts the matching cards aside and ends the turn.

Matching cards show the same value. These are a few examples of possible matches.

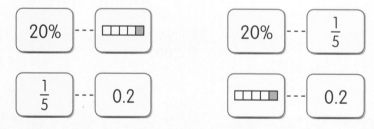

3. Players take turns repeating 2 until there are no cards left in the DRAW pile.

Who is the winner?

The player with the most number of matching cards wins.

INDEPENDENT PRACTICE

Fill in each blank. Express each percent as a fraction in simplest form.

1 $96\% = \dfrac{\boxed{}}{100}$

$= \underline{\hspace{2cm}}$

2 $88\% = \dfrac{\boxed{}}{100}$

$= \underline{\hspace{2cm}}$

3 $42\% = \dfrac{\boxed{}}{100}$

$= \underline{\hspace{2cm}}$

4 $56\% = \dfrac{\boxed{}}{100}$

$= \underline{\hspace{2cm}}$

5 $12\% = \dfrac{\boxed{}}{100}$

$= \underline{\hspace{2cm}}$

6 $78\% = \dfrac{\boxed{}}{100}$

$= \underline{\hspace{2cm}}$

Express each percent as a fraction in simplest form.

7 23%

8 71%

9 2%

10 45%

11 76%

12 54%

Fill in each blank. Express each percent as a decimal.

13 38% = $\dfrac{\boxed{}}{100}$

= _____

14 4% = $\dfrac{\boxed{}}{100}$

= _____

15 97% = $\dfrac{\boxed{}}{100}$

= _____

16 60% = $\dfrac{\boxed{}}{100}$

= _____

Express each percent as a decimal.

17 24%

18 17%

19 69%

20 33%

21 3%

22 80%

Fill in each blank. Express each decimal as a percent.

23 $0.2 = \dfrac{\boxed{}}{10}$

$= \dfrac{\boxed{}}{100}$

$= \underline{\hspace{2cm}}\%$

24 $0.41 = \underline{\hspace{2cm}}$

$= \underline{\hspace{2cm}}\%$

Express each decimal as a percent.

25 0.63

26 0.44

27 0.05

28 0.09

29 0.3

30 0.8

Express each fraction as a percent.

31 $\frac{3}{20}$

32 $\frac{24}{25}$

33 $\frac{9}{50}$

34 $\frac{4}{5}$

35 $\frac{21}{50}$

36 $\frac{78}{200}$

37 $\frac{260}{400}$

38 $\frac{237}{300}$

39 $\frac{35}{125}$

40 $\frac{45}{360}$

Name: _____ Date: _____

3 Percent of a Quantity

Learning Objective:
• Find the value of a percent of a quantity, given the amount and the percent.

💡 THINK

Ms. Walker received a pay raise of 7.5% at the end of the year. Her wage at the beginning of the year was $1,500. How much is her new wage?

ENGAGE

20% of a piece of string is 12 centimeters long. Discuss with your partner what the bar model shows. How can you find the missing lengths in the model?

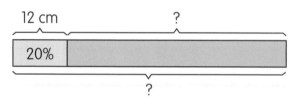

LEARN Find the value of a percent of a quantity

1 Of the 400 seats on an airplane, 80% of the seats are in the economy class cabin. How many seats are in the economy class cabin?

▶ **Method 1**

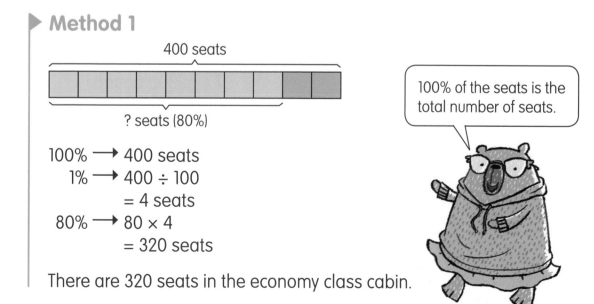

$100\% \longrightarrow 400$ seats
$\quad 1\% \longrightarrow 400 \div 100$
$\qquad = 4$ seats
$\ 80\% \longrightarrow 80 \times 4$
$\qquad = 320$ seats

There are 320 seats in the economy class cabin.

100% of the seats is the total number of seats.

▶ **Method 2**

80% of seats = 80% of 400

$$= \frac{80}{100} \times 400$$

$$= 320$$

There are 320 seats in the economy class cabin.

TRY Practice finding the value of a percent of a quantity

Fill in each blank.

1 Find the value of 20% of 7,500.

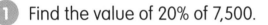

7,500

20%	

?

20% of 7,500 = 20% × _____

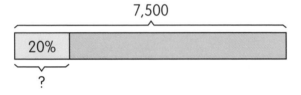

$$= \frac{\boxed{}}{\boxed{}} \times \underline{\hspace{2cm}}$$

$$= \underline{\hspace{2cm}}$$

Solve.

2 90% of 6,300 liters

3 27% of 300 pounds

4 19% of 150 kilometers

5 8% of 465 miles

INDEPENDENT PRACTICE

Solve.

 Find the value of 20% of 800.

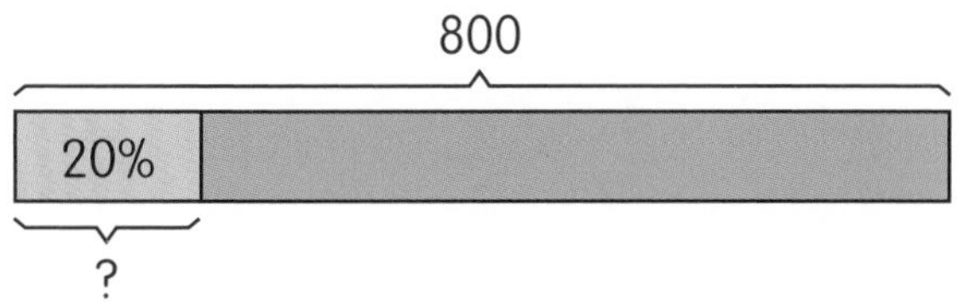

800

| 20% | |

?

 Find the value of 35% of 750.

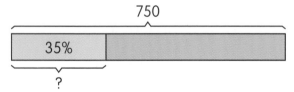

750

| 35% | |

?

Find the value of 82% of 1,360.

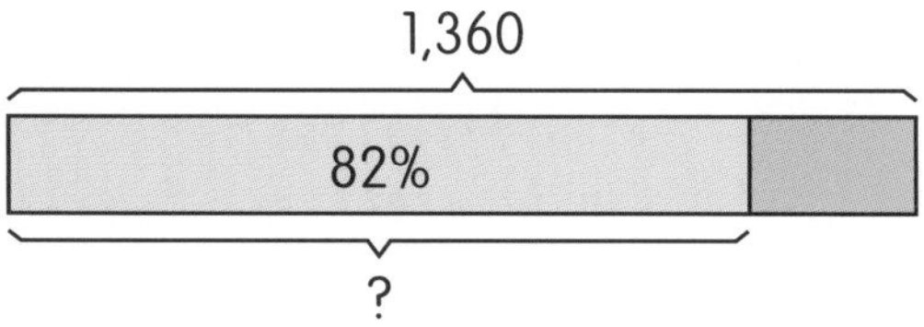

82%

?

Find each value.

 20% of 75 kilograms

5 30% of 80 meters

6 45% of 720 feet

7 62% of 550 gallons

8 40% of 350 grams

9 72% of 800 milliliters

4 Real-World Problems: Percent

Learning Objective:
• Solve real-world problems involving percents.

> **New Vocabulary**
> sales tax   meals tax
> discount   interest

THINK

A baker baked some pies. She sold 90% of the pies at a 40% discount and had 40 pies left. She collected $540 from the sale of her pies. How many pies must she sell at full price to earn the same amount? Explain.

ENGAGE

A watch costs $100 before sales tax. There is a sales tax of 8% on the watch. Haley wants to buy a watch for her mother. How much money will she need to buy the watch? Draw a model to help you.

LEARN Find sales tax

1 A television set costs $1,500. There is a 7% sales tax on the television set. How much is the sales tax?

▶ **Method 1**

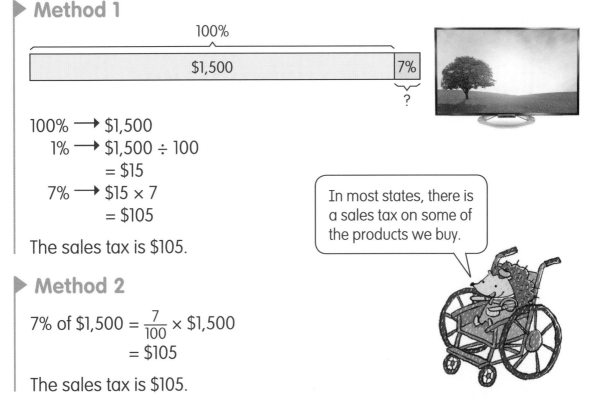

100%

| $1,500 | 7% |

?

100% ⟶ $1,500

1% ⟶ $1,500 ÷ 100
 = $15

7% ⟶ $15 × 7
 = $105

The sales tax is $105.

> In most states, there is a sales tax on some of the products we buy.

▶ **Method 2**

7% of $\$1,500 = \frac{7}{100} \times \$1,500$
$= \$105$

The sales tax is $105.

TRY Practice finding sales tax

Solve. Use the bar model to help you.

1. A video camera cost $820 before sales tax. There was a 6% sales tax on the video camera. How much was the sales tax?

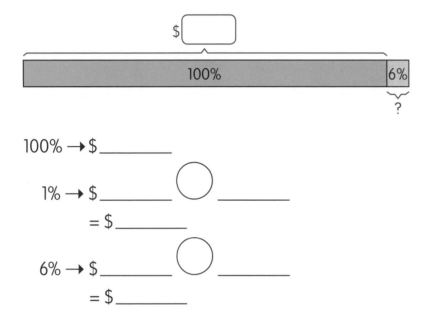

100% → $ _____

1% → $ _____ ◯ _____
  = $ _____

6% → $ _____ ◯ _____
  = $ _____

The sales tax was $ _____.

2. A dress cost $80 before sales tax. There was a 8% sales tax on the dress. How much was the sales tax?

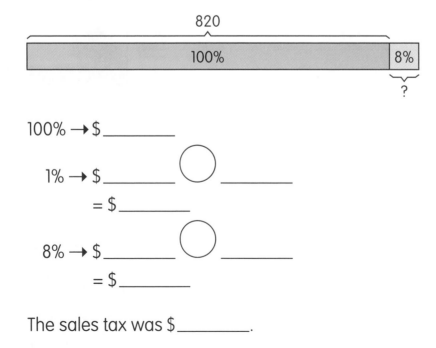

100% → $ _____

1% → $ _____ ◯ _____
  = $ _____

8% → $ _____ ◯ _____
  = $ _____

The sales tax was $ _____.

3 The Carlson family went out to dinner. The cost of the food they ordered was $82. The sales tax of the food was 5%. In addition, they paid a meals tax of 2%. How much was the combined tax?

Combined tax = 5 + 2
            = 7%

A meals tax is applied in addition to a state's sales tax on the purchase of prepared food.

▶ **Method 1**

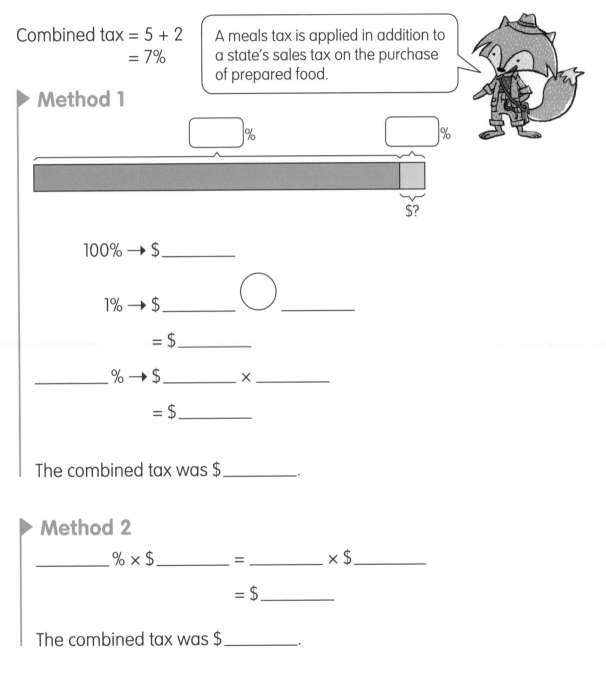

100% → $ _____

1% → $ _____ ◯ _____

     = $ _____

_____ % → $ _____ × _____

     = $ _____

The combined tax was $ _____.

▶ **Method 2**

_____ % × $ _____ = _____ × $ _____

                   = $ _____

The combined tax was $ _____.

ENGAGE

The regular price of a pair of shoes was $80. During a sale, it was sold at 10% less than the regular price. Draw a model to find the cost of the pair of shoes during the sale.

LEARN Find discount

1 The regular price of a sofa was $2,000. During a sale, Mr. Baker bought the sofa at a discount of 15%. What was the dollar amount of the discount?

▶ **Method 1**

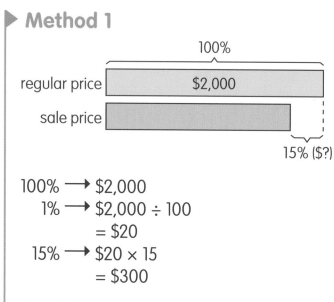

100% ⟶ $2,000

1% ⟶ $2,000 ÷ 100
  = $20

15% ⟶ $20 × 15
  = $300

The dollar amount of the discount was $300.

The discount is the difference between the regular price and the selling price. It is the amount you save.

▶ **Method 2**

Discount = 15% of regular price
  = $\frac{15}{100} \times \$2,000$
  = $300

The dollar amount of the discount was $300.

TRY Practice finding discount

Solve. Use the bar model to help you.

1. The usual price of a refrigerator was $1,800. During a sale, there was a 20% discount on the refrigerator. How much was the discount?

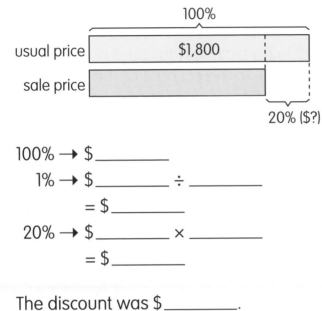

$100\% \rightarrow \$$ _____

$1\% \rightarrow \$$ _____ $\div$ _____

$= \$$ _____

$20\% \rightarrow \$$ _____ $\times$ _____

$= \$$ _____

The discount was $ _____ .

2. An admission ticket to the museum cost $35. Each senior citizen was given a 15% discount. How much was a senior citizen's discount?

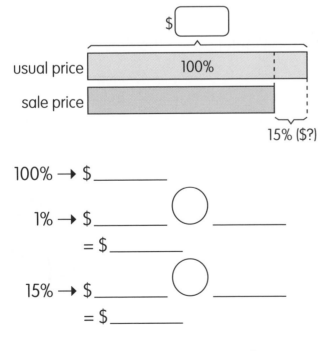

$100\% \rightarrow \$$ _____

$1\% \rightarrow \$$ _____ ◯ _____

$= \$$ _____

$15\% \rightarrow \$$ _____ ◯ _____

$= \$$ _____

A senior citizen's discount was $ _____ .

ENGAGE

Mr. Wood deposited $1,000 in a bank. At the end of a year, the bank gave him 2% of the amount deposited. How much money did Mr. Wood have in the account at the end of the year? Draw a bar model to help you.

LEARN Find interest

1. The Historical Society has $15,000 in an account that pays an interest of 4% per year. How much money will it have in the account at the end of 1 year?

Interest = 4% of $15,000

$$= \frac{4}{100} \times \$15,000$$

$$= \$600$$

> Add the interest to the amount in the account. Interest is the amount that a bank pays you for depositing your money with them.

Amount of money in the account at the end of 1 year
= $15,000 + $600
= $15,600

The Historical Society will have $15,600 in the account at the end of 1 year.

TRY Practice finding interest

Solve. Use the bar model to help you.

1. Daniel took a $20,000 loan from a bank. He paid 6% interest to the bank in the first year. How much interest did Daniel pay in the first year?

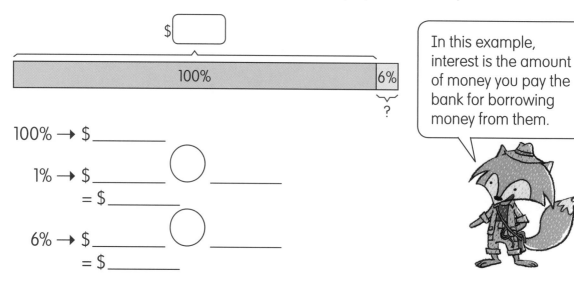

> In this example, interest is the amount of money you pay the bank for borrowing money from them.

100% → $_____

1% → $_____ ◯ _____
= $_____

6% → $_____ ◯ _____
= $_____

Daniel paid $_____ interest in the first year.

ENGAGE

There were 700 people at a musical. 60% of the people were adults. How many children were there? Explain.

LEARN Solve real-world problems involving percents

1. Ms. Torres earns a monthly salary of $4,400. She spends 25% of the salary on rent and 30% of the salary on food. How much of her salary is left?

STEP 1 Understand the problem.

> How much money does Ms. Torres earn a month?
> What percent of the salary does she spend on rent and food?
> What do I need to find?

STEP 2 Think of a plan.
I can draw a bar model.

STEP 3 Carry out the plan.

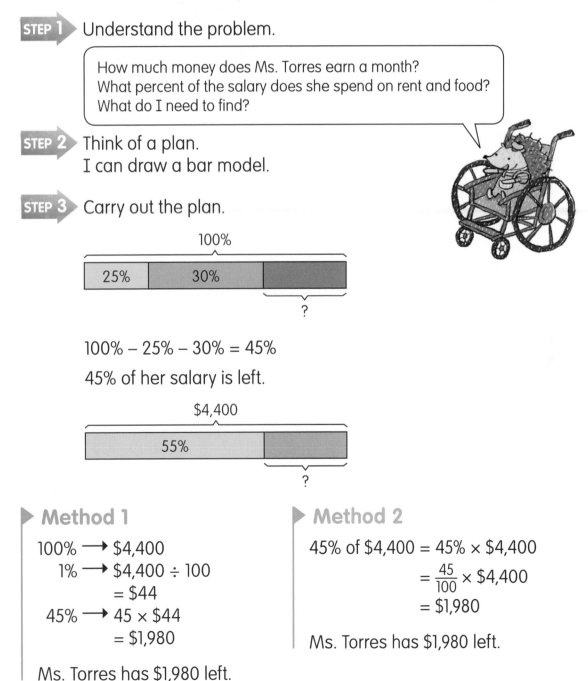

$100\% - 25\% - 30\% = 45\%$

45% of her salary is left.

▶ **Method 1**

$100\% \longrightarrow \$4,400$

$1\% \longrightarrow \$4,400 \div 100$
$ = \$44$

$45\% \longrightarrow 45 \times \$44$
$ = \$1,980$

Ms. Torres has $1,980 left.

▶ **Method 2**

$45\% \text{ of } \$4,400 = 45\% \times \$4,400$
$\phantom{45\% \text{ of } \$4,400} = \frac{45}{100} \times \$4,400$
$\phantom{45\% \text{ of } \$4,400} = \$1,980$

Ms. Torres has $1,980 left.

STEP 4 Check the answer.
I can work backwards to check my answer.

100% → $4,400
   1% → $4,400 ÷ 100
       = $44
  55% → $44 × 55
       = $2,420
$2,420 + $1,980 = $4,400
My answer is correct.

2 A tank was 25% filled with water. The capacity of the tank was 30 liters. How much more water was needed to fill the tank completely?

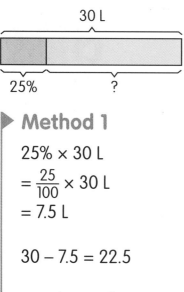

30 L

25%   ?

▶ **Method 1**

25% × 30 L

$= \frac{25}{100} \times 30$ L

$= 7.5$ L

$30 - 7.5 = 22.5$

22.5 liters of water were needed to fill the tank completely.

▶ **Method 2**

$100\% - 25\% = 75\%$

75% × 30 L

$= \frac{75}{100} \times 30$ L

$= 22.5$ L

22.5 liters of water were needed to fill the tank completely.

Work in pairs.

 Write a word problem with some of the words and values given in the box.

sales tax	20%	discount	4%	$5,000
meals tax	7%	interest	$240	$200,000

Example

A company has $200,000 in an investment fund. The fund yields an interest of 4% at the end of each year. How much money did the company have in the fund at the end of 1 year?

Word problem:

2 Ask your partner to use a bar model to solve the problem.

TRY Practice solving real-world problems involving percents

Solve. Use the bar model to help you.

1 A food processor cost $180. Ms Stewart bought it at a discount of 30%. How much did she pay for the food processor?

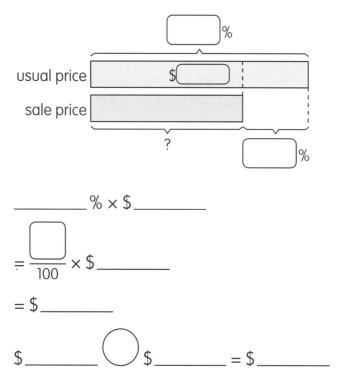

_____ % × $_____

$$= \frac{\boxed{}}{100} \times \$ \underline{\qquad}$$

= $_____

$_____ $\bigcirc$ $_____ = $_____

She paid $_____ for the food processor.

2 A washing machine cost $699 before sales tax. What was the price of the washing machine including a sales tax of 7%?

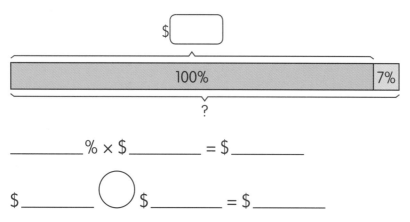

_____ % × $_____ = $_____

$_____ $\bigcirc$ $_____ = $_____

The price of the washing machine including a sales tax of 7% was $_____.

Name: _____ Date: _____

INDEPENDENT PRACTICE

Solve. Draw a bar model to help you.

1 Ms. Ortiz bought a digital camera that cost $320. She paid a sales tax of 5% on the price of the camera. How much sales tax did Ms. Ortiz pay?

2 A restaurant meal for two cost $90. There was a 3% sales tax and a 3% meals tax on the price of the meal. What was the total cost of the meal including the taxes?

3 For a field trip, 35 students went to the zoo. How much did they pay for the tickets in all?

> **Zoo Admission Ticket**
> $15 each
> 20% discount for all students

4 Company ABC invests $185,000 in a fund that pays 6% interest per year. How much money will the company have in the fund at the end of 1 year?

5 Sarah earns $20 a day working after school. She spent 30% of her daily earnings on Monday. How much money was left on Monday?

6 Mr. Green has $4,500 in an account that pays an interest of 3% per year. How much does he have in the account at the end of 1 year?

7. Of the 200 students at Central School, 75% live more than a mile from the school. How many students live a mile or less from the school?

8. The original price of an e-book was $12. It had a discount of 15% during a digital sale. What was the price of the e-book after the discount?

Name: _____ Date: _____

Mathematical Habit 5 Use tools strategically

1 Write a word problem that can be solved using these equations.

$40\% \times 825 = 330$ $\qquad\qquad$ $825 - 330 = 495$

Complete the bar model to solve the problem.

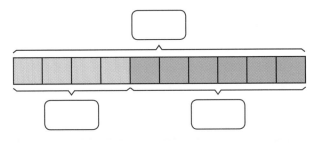

Solve your word problem.

2 The regular price of a jacket was $78. Gabriella bought the jacket at a discount of 5%. How much did she pay for the jacket?

Noah, Micaela and Shanti drew a model each to represent this word problem. Whose bar model is correct? Explain why.

Noah's model

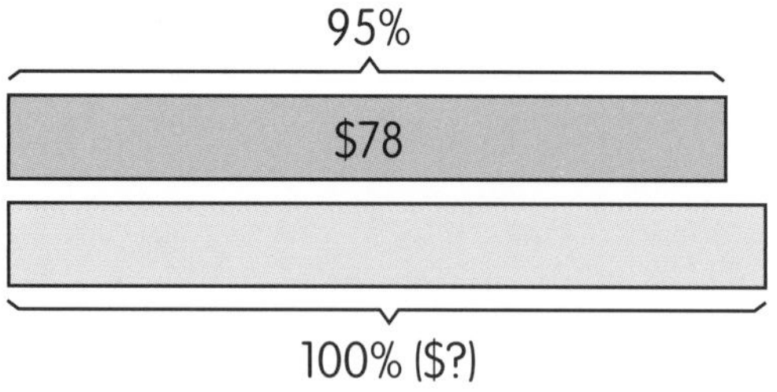

95%

$78

100% ($?)

Micaela's model

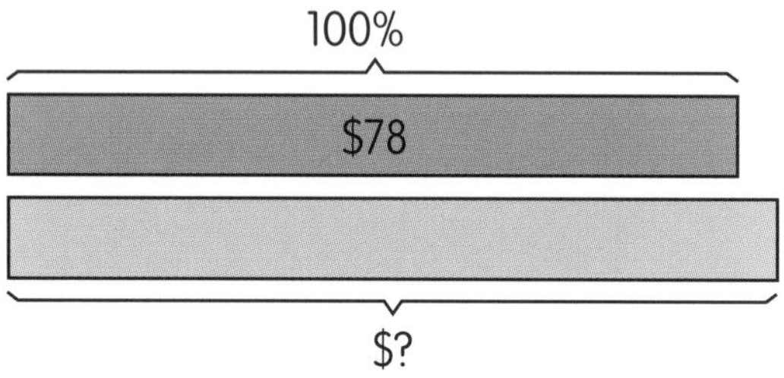

100%

$78

$?

Shanti's model

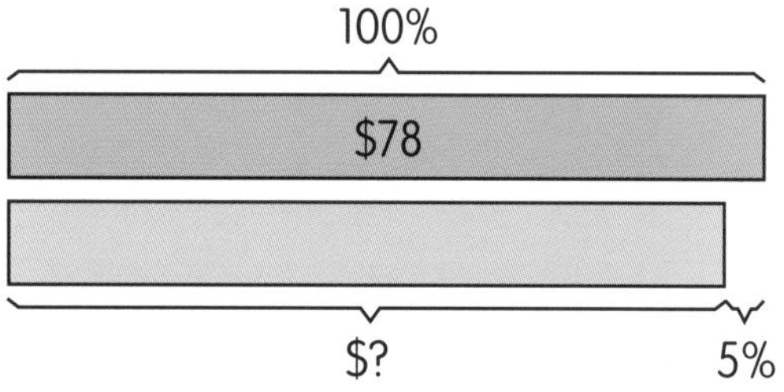

100%

$78

$?   5%

© 2020 Marshall Cavendish Education Pte Ltd

Problem Solving with Heuristics

1 **Mathematical Habit 4** Use mathematical models

In a school fund-raising project, 40% of the total funds collected were from the teachers. Parents and students contributed the remaining amount. The parents contributed twice as much as the students. What percent of the total funds collected was contributed by the students?

2 **Mathematical Habit 1** Persevere in solving problems

The square below is made up of 4 large identical triangles. One of the large triangles has been divided into 4 smaller identical triangles. What percent of the square is shaded?

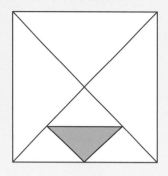

3 **Mathematical Habit** **1** **Persevere in solving problems**

The area of Square A is 64 cm². The area of Rectangle B is 80 cm².
The area of Square A is 4 times the area of the shaded part.
What percent of Rectangle B is shaded?

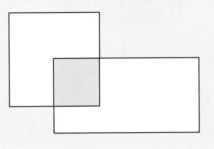

CHAPTER WRAP-UP

 What does percent mean? How can you represent a percent in different ways? How can percents be used in real-world situations?

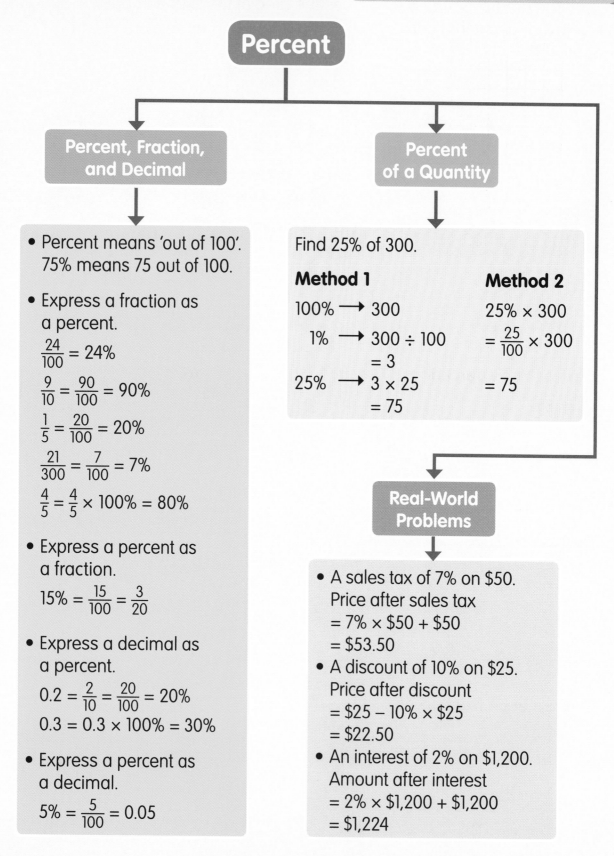

Percent

Percent, Fraction, and Decimal

- Percent means 'out of 100'. 75% means 75 out of 100.

- Express a fraction as a percent.

  $\frac{24}{100} = 24\%$

  $\frac{9}{10} = \frac{90}{100} = 90\%$

  $\frac{1}{5} = \frac{20}{100} = 20\%$

  $\frac{21}{300} = \frac{7}{100} = 7\%$

  $\frac{4}{5} = \frac{4}{5} \times 100\% = 80\%$

- Express a percent as a fraction.

  $15\% = \frac{15}{100} = \frac{3}{20}$

- Express a decimal as a percent.

  $0.2 = \frac{2}{10} = \frac{20}{100} = 20\%$

  $0.3 = 0.3 \times 100\% = 30\%$

- Express a percent as a decimal.

  $5\% = \frac{5}{100} = 0.05$

Percent of a Quantity

Find 25% of 300.

Method 1

100% ⟶ 300

1% ⟶ 300 ÷ 100
     = 3

25% ⟶ 3 × 25
     = 75

Method 2

25% × 300

$= \frac{25}{100} \times 300$

$= 75$

Real-World Problems

- A sales tax of 7% on $50. Price after sales tax
  = 7% × $50 + $50
  = $53.50

- A discount of 10% on $25. Price after discount
  = $25 − 10% × $25
  = $22.50

- An interest of 2% on $1,200. Amount after interest
  = 2% × $1,200 + $1,200
  = $1,224

Name: ____________________ Date: __________

Write each shaded part as a percent of the whole figure.

1. 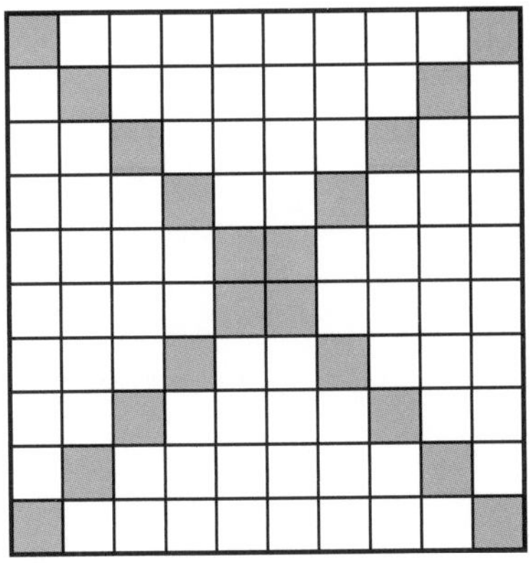 ________

Express as a percent.

2. 45 out of 100

3. 87 out of 100

Express each percent as a fraction in simplest form.

4. 18%

5. 65%

Express each percent as a decimal.

6. 7%

7. 99%

Express each fraction as a percent.

8. $\frac{3}{4}$

9. $\frac{4}{25}$

10. $\frac{84}{400}$

Express each decimal as a percent.

11 0.81

12 0.06

Find each value.

13 52% × 350

14 78% × 650

Solve. Draw a bar model to help you.

15 A laptop costs $1,688 before a sales tax of 9%. What is the price of the laptop including the sales tax?

16 The cost of a dinner at a restaurant is $102. The restaurant charges a sales tax of 3% and a meals tax of 2%. How much was the cost of the dinner after the combined tax?

17 The usual price of an oven was $1,139. During a sale, it was sold at a discount of 15%. How much did the oven cost during the sale?

18 A company invests $500,000 in a fund. The fund yields an interest of 6% at the end of each year. How much will the company have in the fund at the end of the year?

19 The original price of a book was $36. The book was sold at a discount of 10%. What was the price of the book after the discount?

Assessment Prep

Answer each question.

20 Lola has 8 bear figurines. These bear figurines make up 40% of her collection of animal figurines.
Draw a number line to represent the bear figurines and find the total number of animal figurines Lola has.

21 What is 0.07 expressed as a percent?

(A) 0.7%

(B) 7%

(C) 70%

(D) 700%

22 Allison earned a total of $50 from a summer job. She spent 65% of the money on gifts for her family. Then, she spent the rest of the money on a book and a T-shirt. The book cost $7. How much did the T-shirt cost?

Belts on Sale

1 A department store has three types of belts: brown leather, black leather, and decorative metal. Of all the belts, 70% are made of brown leather, 21% are made of black leather, and the remaining 9% are made of decorative metal.

a How many of each type of belt are there?

b 24 more decorative metal belts are delivered to the store before any of the belts are sold. What percent of the total number of belts are decorative metal belts?

2 The regular price of a decorative metal belt is $25. Ariana buys a decorative metal belt at a discount of 25% during a sale.

a   What is the dollar amount of the discount?

b   How much does Ariana pay for the decorative metal belt?

3 Brooke buys a black leather belt that is on sale. The sale price is 10% less than the regular price. The regular price is $3 more than the sale price. There is a 7% sales tax on the regular price of the black leather belt.

a What is the regular price?

b How much is the sales tax?

Rubric

Point(s)	Level	My Performance
7–8	4	• Most of my answers are correct. • I showed complete understanding of what I have learned. • I used the correct strategies to solve the problems. • I explained my answers and mathematical thinking clearly and completely.
5–6.5	3	• Some of my answers are correct. • I showed some understanding of what I have learned. • I used some correct strategies to solve the problems. • I explained my answers and mathematical thinking clearly.
3–4.5	2	• A few of my answers are correct. • I showed little understanding of what I have learned. • I used a few correct strategies to solve the problems. • I explained some of my answers and mathematical thinking clearly.
0–2.5	1	• A few of my answers are correct. • I showed little or no understanding of what I have learned. • I used a few strategies to solve the problems. • I did not explain my answers and mathematical thinking clearly.

Teacher's Comments

Glossary

C

- **composite solid**

  A solid that is made up of two or more basic solids.

- **congruent**

  Two figures that have the same shape and size.

  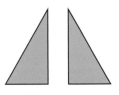

- **coordinate plane**

  A coordinate grid used to locate points in a plane.
  It has a horizontal number line and a vertical number line.

  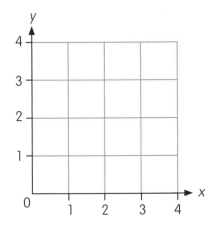

- **coordinates**

  An ordered pair of numbers that gives the location of a point in the coordinate grid.

  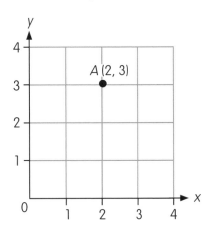

  The coordinates of point A are (2, 3).

D

- **decagon**

  A ten-sided polygon.

- **discount**

  The price difference between the regular price and the selling price.
  It is the amount you save.

E

- **edge**

  The line segment where two faces of a solid figure meet.

  edges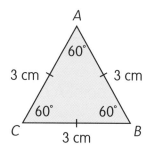

- **equilateral triangle**

  A triangle with all sides of equal length and angle measure.

  ```
        A
       60°
  3 cm    3 cm
     60°   60°
   C         B
      3 cm
  ```

- **equivalent ratios**

  Ratios that represent the same proportional relationship.
  The ratios 1 : 4, 2 : 8, 3 : 12, and 4 : 16 are all equivalent ratios.

H

- **heptagon**

  A seven-sided polygon.

I

- **interest**

  The amount that a bank pays you for depositing your money with them.

- **isosceles triangle**

  A triangle with two sides of equal length and angle measure.

  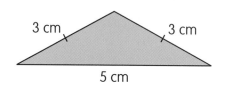

  3 cm   3 cm

  5 cm

K

- **kite**

  A quadrilateral with two pairs of sides of equal length that are adjacent.

  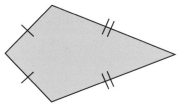

M

- **meals tax**

  A tax applied in addition to a state's sales tax on the purchase of prepared food.

N

- **nonagon**

  A nine-sided polygon.

- **octagon**

  An eight-sided polygon.

O

- **ordered pair**

  A pair of numbers used to name a location on a grid.
  The first number tells the distance from the vertical axis.
  The second number tells the distance from the horizontal axis.
  (2, 3) is the ordered pair for point *A*.

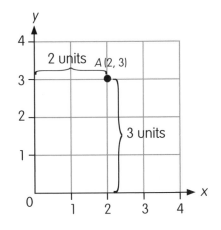

- **origin**

  The point where the *x*- and *y*-axes intersect at right angles in the coordinate plane. The coordinates are (0, 0).

P

- **percent**

  Percent means "out of 100". The symbol for percent is %. 75% means 75 out of 100. Percent can be expressed as a fraction and a decimal.

  $75\% = \frac{75}{100} = 0.75$

R

- **ratio**

  A way of comparing two numbers using division.

  If length A and length B is in the ratio 1 : 3, length A is $1 \div 3 = \frac{1}{3}$ of length B.

- **regular polygon**

  A polygon in which all sides are equal.
  Examples:

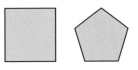

S ———

- **sales tax**

  Tax to pay for items bought in stores. Sales tax rates vary widely across the different states in U.S. The tax rate varies from two to six percent.

- **scalene triangle**

  A triangle with three unequal sides and angles.

  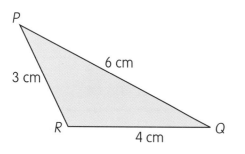

- **Simplest form (of a ratio)**

  A ratio in which the terms have only 1 as a common factor. The simplest form of the ratio 4 : 12 : 8 is 1 : 3 : 2.

T ———

- **term (in a number pattern)**

  Any number in a number pattern. In the number pattern 1, 3, 9, 27 … The first term is 1. The second term is 3. The third term is 9. The fourth term is 27, and so on.

U ———

- **Unit cube**

  A cube in which all edges are 1 unit long.

  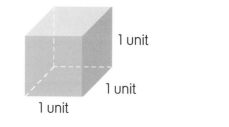

X ———

- **x-axis**

  The horizontal axis on a coordinate grid.

  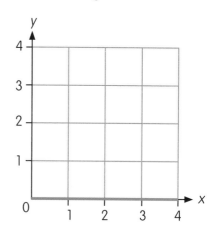

- **x-coordinate**

  The number that is written first in an ordered pair. It tells the distance along the x-axis. In (2, 3), 2 is the x-coordinate.

Y

• **y-axis**

The vertical axis on a coordinate grid.

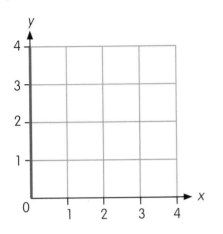

• **y-coordinate**

The number that is written second in an ordered pair.
It tells the distance along the y-axis.
In (2, 3), 3 is the y-coordinate.

Index

Pages in **boldface** type show where a term is introduced.

Edges, *throughout, see for example,* **5**, 42–43, 52, 58, 66

Equilateral triangle, *throughout, see for example,* **123**, 125–130, 132, 137, 140–143

Equivalent fractions
and decimals, 220
using multiplication, 219

Equivalent ratios, **165**, 206
finding, 169
unknown value of, 168, 170, 178–179
using multiplication and division, 167
common factor, 206
writing, 165–166

Figures
three-dimensional, 2

Formula
volume of rectangular prism, 29–31, 54

Fractions
with denominator of 100,
214–215, 233–234
as decimal, 218
equivalent, *see* Equivalent fractions
four operations involving, 72
with line plots, 106
as percents, 232, 234, 236–237, 242,
266–267
percents as, 227–230, 239, 266–267
in simplest form
decimal as, 220
writing, 149
understanding, 148

Graph
on coordinate plane, 83–85
generating patterns and draw, 94, 96, 98

Grid paper, 79

Heptagon, **132**, 140

Hexagon, 123, 132, 140

Hierarchy
polygons and, classification, 131–133, 140

Horizontal number line, 80

100-square grids
pictorial representation, 221–227, 234–235, 269

Interest, **252**, 255, 258–259, 264, 270

Isosceles triangle, *throughout, see for example,* **124**–127, 129–130, 134, 136–137, 140–143

Kite, **132**, 134, 136, 140–142

Line graphs
making and interpreting, 70
pictorial representations, *throughout, see for example,* 70–71, 83–84, 90, 97, 112

Line plots
involving fractional data, 106
making and interpreting, 68, 73–75
pictorial representations, 68–69, 73–75, 106, 108

Liquid
volume of, 3, 28, 54
conversion, 27–28

Liters, *throughout, see for example,* 3–4, 28, 32–35, 37–39, 62

Manipulatives
connecting cubes, *see* Connecting cubes
transparent counters, *see* Transparent counters

R

Ratios, **151**, 206
    bar models to represent, 157
    to compare
        two measurements in same unit, 155–156
        two quantities, 151–152, 206
        two sets of objects, 153–154
        units, 156, 158
    equivalent, *see* Equivalent ratios
    express in simplest form, *throughout, see for example*, 167–168, 176–177, 183–184, 186, 197–199
        three quantities as, 175–177, 179
    part-whole model
        representation, 159
        showing, 159–160
    real-world problems, 185–186, 188, 193
        simplest form to compare quantities, 183–184
    simplifying, 176

Reading, on coordinate plane, 80–81

Real-world problems, 266
    involving percents, 253–254, 256, 266
    ratios, 185–186, 188, 193
        in simplest form to compare quantities, 183–184
    using models to solving, 189
    volume of solid figures to solve, 45–46

Rectangle, *throughout, see for example*, 122, 131–132, 134, 136, 140–143

Rectangular prism
    volume of, *throughout, see for example*, 18–22, 25, 27, 49, 54
        formula, 29–31, 54
        solid composed of two, 44

Regular polygon, **131**, 133, 135, 141

Rhombus, *throughout, see for example*, 122, 131–132, 134, 136–137, 140–143

Right triangle, 105, 120–121, 137, 140–141

S

Sales tax, *throughout, see for example*, **247**–248, 255–257, 266, 268–269, 275

Scalene triangle, *throughout, see for example*, **124**–125, 127, 132, 136–137, 140–143

Simplest form
    fractions
        expressed in, 219, 227–230
        writing in, 149
    ratios, **167**, 206
        to compare quantities in real-world problems, 183–184
        expressed, *throughout, see for example*, 167–168, 176–177, 183–184, 186, 197–199

Solids, 54
    comparing, 7–8
    using unit cubes, 5–7
    volume of, 8, 54
        in cubic units, 11–12, 14–16
        to solve real-world problems, 45–46

Square, *throughout, see for example*, 5, 61, 132, 134, 140

Subtraction
    comparing numbers using, 148

Tables
    pictorial representations, *throughout, see for example*, 22, 68–71, 83– 85, 92–94, 125

Tally charts
    pictorial representations, 68–69, 75, 103

Term
    in a number pattern, *throughout, see for example*, **91**–93, 96–97, 100, 102, 104–105

Three-dimensional figures, 2

Three quantities
    as ratios, 175–177, 179, 206

Three-step word problems, 36–37

Transparent counters
    manipulatives, 151–153, 165

Trapezoid, *throughout, see for example*, 122, 132, 134, 136–137, 140–143

Triangles
    acute, 105, 120–121, 132, 140
    classification, 120–121, 123, 125
        identification and, 123–124, 126
    equilateral, *throughout, see for example,* **123**,
        125–130, 132, 137, 140–143
    isosceles, *throughout, see for example,* **124**–127,
        129–130, 134, 136–137, 140–143
    obtuse, *throughout, see for example,* 120–121,
        125, 132, 134, 140
    right, *throughout, see for example,* 105, 120–121,
        137, 140–141
    scalene, *throughout, see for example,* **124**–125,
        127, 132, 136–137, 140–143

Two-step word problems, 34–35

Unit cubes, **5**, 54
    build
        different solids, 6
        solid using, 5–7
    counting number of, 11–12
    least number of, 53

Unknown value
    of equivalent ratios, 168, 170, 178–179

Vertical number line, 80

Volume, 54
    composite solids, **44**, 54
    of cube, 15
    difference between, 49
    formula for, 19, 29, 31, 54

of liquid, 3, 28, 54
    conversion, 27–28
measurements, 15
    capacity and, 3
of rectangular prism, *throughout, see for
    example,* 18–22, 25, 27, 49, 54
    formula, 29–31
of solids, 8, 54
    in cubic units, 11–12, 14–16
    to solve real-world problems, 45–46

Whole numbers, 106

Word problems
    one-step, 32–33
    three-step, 36–37
    two-step, 34–35

Writing
    equivalent ratios, 165–166
    fractions in simplest form, 149

x-axis, **80**, 82–83, 106, 113

x-coordinate, **80**, 83, 106, 113

Y

y-axis, **80**, 82–83, 106, 113

y-coordinate, **80**, 83, 106, 113

Photo Credits

1: © MAX BLENDER 3D/Shutter Stock, 1t: © Georgii Dolgykh/123rf.com, 1m: © Igor Zakharevich/123rf.com, 1b: © Igor Zakharevich/123rf.com, 8tl: © Gennaro86/Dreamstime.com, 8tr: © monbibi/Shutter Stock, 8ml: © akulamatiau/123rf.com, 8mr: © Anton Starikov/Dreamstime.com, 8bl: © Lightkitegirl/Dreamstime.com, 8br: © Mikhail Kokhanchikov/Dreamstime.com, 10tl: © Alexapicso/Shutter Stock, 10tr: © Athomas Athomas/Dreamstime.com, 10ml: © Pagina/Shutter Stock, 10mr: © Prillfoto/Dreamstime.com, 10bl: © Skypixel/Dreamstime.com, 10br: © Peter Baxter/Shutter Stock, 49: Created by Fwstudio - Freepik.com, 66tr: © supermimicry/Shutter Stock, 66mr: © Dsapach/Dreamstime.com, 66br: © Pikepicture/Dreamstime.com, 67: © Alf Ribeiro/Shutter Stock, 88: © piotr_pabijan/Shutter Stock, 103: Created by Fwstudio - Freepik.com, 119: © malija/123rf.com, 119m: © Jan Janu/Dreamstime.com, 128bl: © Vitezslav Valka/Shutter Stock, 137: Created by Fwstudio - Freepik.com, 146(tr to br): i) © Lubov Dubikova/Dreamstime.com, ii) © Lubov Dubikova/Dreamstime.com, iii) © Seijiro/Dreamstime.com, iv) © Petr Vaclavek/Dreamstime.com, 147t: © redhayabusa/123rf.com, 147m: © Paolo De Santis/123rf.com, 147ml: © Евгений Косцов/123rf.com, 147bl: © Kwanchai Lerttanapunyaporn/123rf.com, 147b: © rusrf/123rf.com, 151ml: © MCE, 151bl: © Prapan Ngawkeaw/123rf.com, 151br: © Pavel Lipskiy/123rf.com, 152t: © MCE, 152bl: © MCE, 153t: © MIKHAIL GRACHIKOV/123rf.com, 153m: © MCE, 153b: © Okeat/Dreamstime.com, 153bl: © Lobeart/Dreamstime.com, 153br: © Anphotost/Dreamstime.com, 155t: © utima/123rf.com, 155t: © photomaru/iStock.com, 156ml: © Pixelrobot/Dreamstime.com, 156bl: © Wachira Sonwongsa/123rf.com, 157mm: © MCE, 159bl: © MCE, 161t: © tissansk/123rf.com, 161ml: © Borys Shevchuk/123rf.com, 161mr: © boule13/123rf.com, 163tl: © Pavel Lipskiy/123rf.com, 163tr: © Paperkites/iStock.com, 163ml: © Oleg Vydyborets/123rf.com, 163m: © Michael Fair/123rf.com, 165ml: © MCE, 165(m to b): i) © Elena Schweitzer/Dreamstime.com, ii) © Viktor Prymachenko/ Dreamstime.com, iii) © koosen/123rf.com, 165(t to m): i) © Elena Schweitzer/Dreamstime.com, ii) © Viktor Prymachenko/ Dreamstime.com, iii) © koosen/123rf.com, 169: © MCE, 172: © piotr_pabijan/Shutter Stock, 175b: i) © cosmin4000/iStock.com, ii) © Prapass Wannapinij/t/Dreamstime.com, iii) © Meysam Rezvani Abkenarit/Dreamstime.com, 177tl: © MCE, 188b: © Jan Marijs/123rf.com, 196b: © nazdravie/123rf.com, 197br: © nitr/123rf.com, 199br: © Konstantinfotografov2012t/Dreamstime.com, 200br: © siraphol/123rf.com, 203: Created by Fwstudio - Freepik.com, 207t: © Wattanaphob Kappago/123rf.com, 209br: © Andrii Gorulko/123rf.com, 216tr: © Weera Namkhatet/Dreamstime.com, 216mr: © Andrew Balcombet/Dreamstime.com, 217: © Clearvista/Dreamstime.com, 224br: © conneldesign/123rf.com, 238: © piotr_pabijan/Shutter Stock, 244tr: © Boyarkinamarina/Dreamstime.com, 247mr: © Chakrapong Worathat/123rf.com, 256tr: © Ansis Klucis/123rf.com, 261: Created by Fwstudio - Freepik.com, 268mr: © scanrail/123rf.com

NOTES

NOTES

NOTES

NOTES

© 2020 Marshall Cavendish Education Pte Ltd

Published by Marshall Cavendish Education
Times Centre, 1 New Industrial Road, Singapore 536196
Customer Service Hotline: (65) 6213 9688
US Office Tel: (1-914) 332 8888 | Fax: (1-914) 332 8882
E-mail: cs@mceducation.com
Website: www.mceducation.com

Distributed by
Houghton Mifflin Harcourt
125 High Street
Boston, MA 02110
Tel: 617-351-5000
Website: www.hmhco.com/programs/math-in-focus

First published 2020

ISBN 978-0-358-10187-1

Printed in Singapore

3 4 5 6 7 8 9   1401   26 25 24 23 22 21
4500817280   B C D E F

The cover image shows a giant panda.
Giant pandas have thick, fluffy, black and white fur. They live in bamboo forests in China. Bamboo accounts for over 95% of their diet. Unlike other bears, pandas do not hibernate in the winter. They migrate to areas with warmer temperatures depending on the season. They used to be endangered in the past, but are now protected and their numbers are increasing once again.